THIS PAGE:
Ypsilon Mountain, Rocky Mountain NP.

ON THE COVER:
Alpine Tundra looking west to the Never Summer
Range, Rocky Mountain NP

Photos by: NPS and Josh Heise

Rocky Mountain National Park

Geologic Resource Evaluation Report

Natural Resource Report NPS/NRPC/GRD/NRR—2004/004

Geologic Resources Division
Natural Resource Program Center
P.O. Box 25287
Denver, Colorado 80225

September 2004

U.S. Department of the Interior
Washington, D.C.

The Natural Resource Publication series addresses natural resource topics that are of interest and applicability to a broad readership in the National Park Service and to others in the management of natural resources, including the scientific community, the public, and the NPS conservation and environmental constituencies. Manuscripts are peer-reviewed to ensure that the information is scientifically credible, technically accurate, appropriately written for the intended audience, and is designed and published in a professional manner.

Natural Resource Reports are the designated medium for disseminating high priority, current natural resource management information with managerial application. The series targets a general, diverse audience, and may contain NPS policy considerations or address sensitive issues of management applicability. Examples of the diverse array of reports published in this series include vital signs monitoring plans; "how to" resource management papers; proceedings of resource management workshops or conferences; annual reports of resource programs or divisions of the Natural Resource Program Center; resource action plans; fact sheets; and regularly-published newsletters.

Views and conclusions in this report are those of the authors and do not necessarily reflect policies of the National Park Service. Mention of trade names or commercial products does not constitute endorsement or recommendation for use by the National Park Service.

Printed copies of reports in these series may be produced in a limited quantity and they are only available as long as the supply lasts. This report is also available from the Geologic Resource Evaluation Program website (http://www2.nature.nps.gov/geology/inventory/ gre_publications) on the internet, or by sending a request to the address on the back cover. Please cite this publication as:

KellerLynn, K. 2004. Rocky Mountain National Park Geologic Resource Evaluation Report. Natural Resource Report NPS/NRPC/GRD/NRR—2004/004. National Park Service, Denver, Colorado.

NPS D-307, September 2004

Table of Contents

Executive Summary 1

Dedication and Acknowledgements 2

Introduction 3
   Purpose of the Geologic Resources Evaluation Program..3
   Geologic Setting 3

Geologic Issues 5
   Alpine Environments..5
   Flooding...5
   Hydrogeology 6
   Mass Wasting 7
   Minerals and Mining 8
   Seismicity 9
   Water Diversion Projects 10
   Wind-Blown Sediment 10
   Potential Research, Inventory, and Monitoring Projects 11

Geologic Features and Processes 14
   Colorado River...14
   Columnar Jointing..14
   Exfoliation Domes and Ornate Erosion Features...14
   Glacial Features 14
   Glaciers 15
   Lakes 16
   Meandering Streams 16
   Patterned Ground 16
   Sackung 17
   Solifluction 17
   Tors 17
   Uplifted Erosion Surface..17

Formation Properties 19
   Formation Properties Table 20

Geologic History.. 23

References Cited 26

Appendix A: Geologic Map Graphic 30
Appendix B: Evaluation of Comprehensive Interpretive Plan (2001)....................... 31

Attachment 1: Digital Geologic Map (CD)

Executive Summary

The geologic features of Rocky Mountain National Park have long been under the careful scrutiny of many geologists. From their studies a great deal is known of the history, which is full of interesting events and shifting scenes. The park's long geologic story continues today with geologic processes changing the present landscape.

Three compelling stories encapsulate the nearly two-billion- year- old history of the park. The first story takes place during Precambrian time. This tale highlights the themes of "deep time" and understanding the origins of our physical surroundings, and perhaps our place in the world. The ancient metamorphic and igneous rocks—most of which are between 1.4 and 1.7 billion years old—in the park serve as a physical backdrop for this story.

The second story is much more recent. Between 23 and 29 million years ago, during the Oligocene Epoch the park was the scene of widespread volcanic activity. As uplift of the region continued throughout the Tertiary Period, volcanoes erupted, ash filled the air, faults formed, and granitic magma intruded what are now the Never Summer Mountains. The tale provides a sense of shifting scenes throughout time. A hike through Little Yellowstone on the west side of the park serves as a backdrop for this story. There are also roadside locations for telling this story, such as Lava Cliffs and Gore Range Overlook.

The third story is an ice age one. The story of glaciation in Rocky Mountain National Park is still unfolding. The main characters left quite a bit of evidence, but geologists are still working out the timing of events. Two major valley glaciations, a smaller cirque glaciation, and periods of ice accumulation are recorded in the park. The two Pleistocene glaciations, Bull Lake and Pinedale, produced the rugged look of the topographic features of today's high country. Many of the distinctive geologic features found throughout the park have a glacial origin. (See Geologic Features and Processes section of this report.)

The park's geologic story continues to the present, with human activities influencing natural processes. Park planning must address development in high alpine environments: frost cracking and solifluction are two processes that require attention. The particular hydrogeology of the park and associated floods, water quality, and wetlands are important issues for planning, visitor safety, protection of resources, and compliance with section 404 of the Clean Water Act and the NPS Director's Order #77- 1 (the policy directive addressing wetland protection in the National Park System). Notably human activities have impacted the park's

hydrogeology more water diversion projects than all other national parks combined.

Although addressed in the late 1980s and early 1990s, an understanding of the park's mining history is important for resource protection and visitor safety. Managers have gated mine openings with bat- friendly (not visitor-friendly) entrances, but an awareness of the locations of minerals (and possibly fossils) is important for resource protection.

Park managers may also wish to take note of areas susceptible to mass wasting, including landslides, debris flows, rockfalls, and snow avalanches, because of human influences on these processes and visitor safety. In some cases, such as the "Holzwarth debris flow," human activities (i.e., the diversion of water in the Grand Ditch) are a likely influence on the lobate mass of material deposited on the west side of the Kawuneeche Valley. No single mechanism causes slope failure, but researchers suggest that freeze- thaw processes cause rockfalls that form talus deposits at the base of all steep slopes in the park. The combination of areal extent and visitor safely makes mass wasting a significant geologic issue for the park.

Less conspicuous than talus, although no less important with respect to sediment distribution, is wind- blown detritus. Wind- blown sediment is the dominant sediment source for alpine lakes in Colorado (Caine, 1974). Aeolian dust is transported through alpine hillslope systems and is stored in alpine lakes and tundra soils (Caine, 1986). In the context of the park's close proximity to metropolitan areas of the Front Range, this information is significant with respect to incoming pollutants, such as nitrogen.

Finally, although the park is in a zone of minor seismic hazard, similar to most mountainous areas in Colorado, the largest historical earthquake in Colorado occurred in the vicinity of Estes Park. This earthquake predates seismographs, so an estimated magnitude of 6.5 is based on the size of the area over which the earthquake was felt (Colorado Geological Survey, unpublished data, 1999). A large earthquake near the park could cause rockfalls and landslides, and changes in springs and streamflow (Geoindicators report, unpublished data, 2001).

Dedication and Acknowledgements

William Alfred Braddock
February 3, 1929–January 1, 2003

Bill Braddock's professional career spanned more than 40 years and combined his life- long interests of geologic structures, teaching and training students in the challenging area of field investigations, and hiking in the high country of Colorado's Front Range. Bill's research contributions include the *Geologic Map of Rocky Mountain National Park and Vicinity, Colorado.*

Colleagues remember Bill as providing "guidance, counsel, and friendship," as a "born teacher," as "one of the best minds in the [University of Colorado Geology] department," and one of the "best field geologists."

Bill's desire and gift for teaching extended beyond his 36 years at the University of Colorado, particularly in connection with his geologic studies in Rocky Mountain National Park. He volunteered countless hours over many years to provide geology training for seasonal interpreters, to lead field trips, to conduct geology seminars for the Rocky Mountain Nature Association, and to provide counsel to park resource managers on geologic matters. This report represents the last geologic review he provided. His dedication and concern for park science continued until his death and will be appreciated far beyond.

Acknowledgements

In addition to staff at the NPS Geologic Resource Division, the following individuals deserve to be acknowledged with respect to their assistance with this report. Thanks to Bill Braddock, Jim Cole, and Rich Madole for their guidance and input during the overall review of the report. Larry Martin and Vince Matthews provided information on the park's hydrogeology and structural geology, respectively. Kevin C. "Casey" McKinney provided insight into the potentially fossiliferous outcrops of the Troublesome Formation in the park. Also, thanks to park staff members, Larry Frederick for the opportunity to review the park's comprehensive interpretation plan with respect to geology, and Terry Terrill for providing information on the park's research needs.

Introduction

Geologic resources serve as the foundation of park ecosystems, as such an understanding of these resources is needed for informed decision making in parks.

Purpose of the Geologic Resources Evaluation Program

The NPS Natural Resource Challenge—an action plan to advance the management and protection of park resources—has focused efforts to inventory the natural resources of parks. A geologic inventory is administered by the Geologic Resources Division through the Geologic Resource Evaluation (GRE) Program. The goal of the GRE Program is to provide each of the identified 274 "natural area" parks with a digital geologic map, a geologic evaluation report, and a geologic bibliography. Each product is a tool to support the stewardship of park resources and each is designed to be user friendly to non- geoscientists.

The GRE teams hold scoping meetings at parks to review available data on the geology of a particular park and to discuss the geologic issues in the park. During these meetings park staffs are afforded the opportunity to meet with experts on the geology of their park. Scoping meetings are usually held individually in each park, which permits a focused discussion and exploration of available information on a park's resources. However, some scoping meetings involve multiple parks or an entire Vital Signs Monitoring Network to expedite the inventory process.

Geologic Setting

Looking west from Denver the Front Range rises from the plains in two giant steps: first the foothills that climb above the "Mile High City," then the high alpine summits, 54 of which loom above 14,000 feet (4,267 m). The difference in elevation between the peaks and nearby lowlands is striking. The square- topped silhouette of Longs Peak (14,256 ft, 4,345 m), the highest mountain in Rocky Mountain National Park, is the northernmost "fourteener" (mountains that exceed 14,000 feet above sea level) and towers 9,000 feet (2,743 m) above the adjacent plain. Longs Peak, a mass of Precambrian Silver Plume Granite, has challenged climbers since 1868 when a small party, that included John Wesley Powell, made the first recorded ascent. The infamous Diamond of Longs Peak, which ranks as the largest, highest, and steepest wall in the Southern Rockies, remains alluring to technical rock climbers from around the world.

The high country of the park consists of mountain peaks ranging in elevation from 11,000 to 14,000 feet (3,350 to 4,270 m) above sea level that form the Continental Divide, Trail Ridge, the Mummy Range, and the Never Summer Mountains. In addition to their height, the age of the rocks that form the core of these mountains is impressive. Although not the oldest rock in the National Park System (Grand Teton National Park holds that honor), they are from the same geologic time span, the Precambrian, which contains the oldest rocks on Earth and harkens back to a time when Earth's early crust and continents were forming. Volcanism formed much younger rocks (23 to 29 million years ago), which lie on the western slope of the park and constitute much of the Never Summer Mountains.

Much of the high country consists of gently rolling topography into which glaciers have cut cirques and valleys. Although the rocks that comprise the range are ancient, the timing of its uplift makes the Southern Rockies geologic newcomers as compared to mountain ranges such as the Appalachians. Like the ranges that were here before them, the Rockies began their rise from the bed of an ancient sea, but in this case just 70 million years ago during a period of mountain building called the Laramide orogeny. The north- south trending Front Range is principally the result of Laramide mountain building, faulting, and subsequent erosion. Present- day relief was enhanced by additional uplift during Cenozoic time (the most recent geologic era).

The Front Range contains some of the most accessible alpine scenery in the Southern Rockies. Rocky Mountain National Park preserves thousands of acres of mountain meadows, snow- fed streams, rolling alpine uplands, glacial moraines and valleys, volcanoes, lava, and ash. Trail Ridge Road traverses 50 miles (80 km) of rugged, mountain terrain between the resort communities of Estes Park and Grand Lake. The 11- mile (18- km) section of road that lies above tree line follows the Continental Divide and winds through periglacial environments covered by alpine tundra. More than 300 miles (483 km) of hiking trails provide access from roadways and trailheads to remote areas of the park.

Rocks and deposits are the foundation of today's scenery and record the geologic history and evolution of the park, which spans nearly two billion years. The evolution of the park's landscape may be highlighted with these geologic events:

Precambrian Time
- Sediment deposited in an ancient sea (1,800 to 2,000 million years ago)
- Sedimentary and volcanic rocks metamorphosed into biotite schist and biotite gneiss (1,750 million years ago)
- Intrusion of Boulder Creek Granordiorite (1,664 million years ago)

- Intrusion of granitic batholiths: Hagues Peak Granite (1,480 million years ago) and Silver Plume Granite (1,420 million years ago)
- Intrusion of the Iron Dike (1,317 million years ago)
- Erosion of mountains (1,300 to 500 million years ago)

Paleozoic and Mesozoic Eras
- Shallow sea covered the area (500 to 300 million years ago)
- Accumulation of marine sediments on beveled Precambrian mountains
- Intrusion of kimberlites (probably during the Devonian Period, 417 to 354 million years ago)
- Formation of the Ancestral Rocky Mountains (300 million years ago) and erosion of pre- Mississippian-age cover
- Intermittent inundation by seas (Permian to Cretaceous, 286 to 65 million years ago)
- Deposition of marine, fluvial, and aeolian deposits
- Beginning of Laramide orogeny (70 million years ago, Late Cretaceous)
- Withdrawal of seas

Cenozoic Era
- Laramide orogeny continues (including uplift, volcanism, erosion, fluvial deposition)
- Ongoing erosion (Mesozoic strata stripped away, exposing Precambrian rocks)
- Intrusion of granitic magmas and eruption of lava flows and ash (29 to 23 million years ago)
- Continued erosion; uplift, broad up- arching, and block faulting
- Canyon cutting (continues to present)
- Global climate cooling (beginning timing unknown, possibly about 2.5–2.6 million years ago; major climatic cooling by 800,000 years ago)
- Glaciation: Bull Lake (beginning timing unknown to about 127,000 years ago) and Pinedale (beginning about 30,000 years ago; glacial maximum between 23,500 and 20,000 years ago; 15,000 and 12,000 years ago deglaciation occurred; prior to 10,000 years ago, all Pinedale glaciers disappeared)
- Neoglaciation (about 5,000 to 120 years ago)
- Geomorphic processes continue to affect the present landscape

Geologic Issues

This section identifies geologic issues that may warrant attention from resource managers in Rocky Mountain National Park. These issues are relevant for maintenance of facilities, mitigation of hazardous conditions, and protection of resources.

Alpine Environments

Frost Cracking

Frost cracks are common features in alpine areas. They occur in turf-banked lobes and terraces. Frost cracking has the potential to create significant engineering and maintenance problems at high elevations. Investigators studied frost cracking at high elevations (approximately 11,500 ft; 3,505 m) on Niwot Ridge, south of the park in the Indian Peaks Wilderness (Benedict, 1970). The mean annual air temperature during the study was 26°F (-3°C), with 12-year temperature extremes of -34°F (-37°C) and 67°F (19°C). Annual precipitation during this interval ranged from a minimum of 19 inches (48 cm) to a maximum of 32 inches (81 cm). Because of the close proximity and similar environment, information gained from this study may be useful for park managers in Rocky Mountain National Park.

Frost cracks are variable both in size and appearance. Some are only hairline fissures in the turf, whereas others are 8 to 12 inches (20 to 30 cm) wide. The sides of frost cracks are generally free of vegetation and have been churned by needle ice and microsolifluction. Single cracks are most common, but sub-parallel and irregularly branching cracks also occur. The largest cracks are more than 150 feet (46 m) in length (Benedict, 1970).

Frost cracks occur only where heaving is intense and varies within short horizontal distances, such as on turf-banked lobes and terraces, frost boils, and areas that are temporarily domed upward by localized heaving. Frost cracks either cannot form, or else are not preserved, in areas where solifluction is intense (Benedict, 1970).

In general, frost cracks are seasonal and begin to open as soon as soil starts to freeze and expand (in November during the study on Niwot Ridge). Cracks continue to expand as long as heaving continues. The cracks begin to close with the arrival of above-freezing temperatures, but may reopen during brief intervals of renewed freezing (mid-May).

Solifluction

Identifying high-elevation areas with active solifluction—slow soil movement in periglacial areas—and incorporating that information into the park's GIS would be useful to park managers, including maintenance staff. Periglacial landscapes with active soil flowage can create significant engineering and maintenance problems for facilities, roads, trails, and septic systems. Sections of Trail Ridge Road, which cross slopes with active soil flowage, have significant and recurring maintenance problems (Geoindicators report, unpublished data, 2001). The rates of flowage have fluctuated throughout geologic time, and some change is expected. However, the combination of building the road across this terrain and loading the slope with roadfill material may have changed the rate of movement in these areas.

Flooding

Flash flooding is extremely rare at high elevations (above about 7,500 ft, 2,286 m) (Jarrett, 1987), but storm-related flooding is not uncommon in the Front Range. Floods have produced marked geologic and geomorphic changes.

Big Thompson Flood

No previous historic flood involved as much erosion and material transport as the Big Thompson River flood of 1976 (Shroba and others, 1979). Because of its close proximity to the park and the fact that the headwaters originate there, this flood warrants mention. Exceptionally heavy summer rainfall, due to a persistent weather system over a few days, caused this event. Damage caused by the flood largely occurred east of Rocky Mountain National Park and downstream from Lake Estes.

The Big Thompson River initiates near timerline just below the Continental Divide at an altitude of about 11,000 feet (3,350 m). Some of its tributaries arise even higher from small glaciers (Shroba and others, 1979). The headwaters are rimmed on the west, north, and south by peaks that stand more than 12,000 feet (3,660) in elevation. The Big Thompson River descends about 6,330 feet (1,930 m) in 55 miles (88 km)—as the crow flies—from its sources to its confluence with the South Platte River on the Great Plains at an altitude of about 4,670 feet (1,420 m). The Big Thompson River descends about 3,500 feet (1,065 m) in 17 miles (27 km) as it flows eastward from its source to the Town of Estes Park at the west edge of the downpour area of the Big Thompson River flood (Shroba and others, 1979).

The Big Thompson storm and flood of 1976 were exceptional but not unique events. Comparable storms and floods have happened in the Front Range in the past and probably will happen in the future (Shroba and others, 1979). Intense rainfall from the Big Thompson thunderstorm complex on the evening of July 31, 1976, and the ensuing floods that evening and following day led to widespread erosion and deposition along the Big Thompson River and its tributaries. Because of the intensity of the rainfall and the steepness of the terrain, runoff quickly reached flood stage.

The main channel was scoured throughout its length. Point bars formed where the gradient flattened at wide places on the floodplain and on the insides of bends. Large boulder- gravel bars diverted the river from its pre- flood channel, notably at the community of Drake. Where bridges, buildings, or vegetation impeded flow, deposition intensified. Boulders as large as 7 feet (2.1 m) in intermediate diameter were deposited in bars. The largest boulder apparently moved by the flood measured approximately 12- by- 12- by- 23 feet (4- by- 4- by- 7 m) and weighed an estimated 275 tons (250 t) (Shroba and others, 1979).

Downstream from the mouth of the canyon, overbank deposition was the chief geologic effect of the flood, although scour was appreciable at the outsides of bends and in the main channel (Shroba and others, 1979). Sheetflooding on hillslopes locally removed as much as a foot (30 cm) of soil and left pebbly to boulderly lag deposits. Locally, sheetflooding transported boulders down slopes, which were deposited on gentler inclines (Shroba and others, 1979). Debris slides, debris flows, rockslides, and rockfalls were set off in the intense-downpour area. Saturation of the soil was the chief cause, but lateral undercutting did cause some landslides (Shroba and others, 1979).

Lawn Lake Flood
At approximately 0530 Mountain Daylight Time on the morning of July 15, 1982, Lawn Lake dam failed. The dam was a 79- year- old (Pitlick, 1993b), 26- foot (7.9- m) high earthen dam (Jarrett and Costa, 1986) near the head of the Roaring River valley. The dam released 674 acre- feet (831,716 m³) of water and an estimated peak discharge of 18,000 cubic feet (509,760 dm³) per second (Jarrett and Costa, 1986). By comparison, investigators estimate the "500 year flood" in this area to have peak discharges of only about 400 cubic feet (11,330 dm³) per second (Hoyt, 1987). Thus the hydrologic consequences of the Lawn Lake dam failure were truly exceptional, and peak discharges of the flood far exceeded naturally occurring flows (Pitlick, 1993a).

The flood caused the death of three people and property damage totaling $31 million. The Colorado State Engineer determined that the probable cause of failure was deterioration of lead caulking used for the connection between the outlet pipe and the gate valve. The resulting leak eroded the earthfill of the dam. Continued erosion by percolating water led to progressive formation of narrow conduits or "pipes," and ultimately to failure of the embankment (Jarrett and Costa, 1986).

Floodwater from the Lawn Lake discharge overtopped Cascade Lake dam, located 6.7 miles (11 km) downstream. With 4.2 feet (1.3 m) of water flowing over its crest, Cascade Lake dam failed by toppling. The flood continued down Fall River into the Town of Estes Park, where overbank flow caused extensive damage (Jarrett and Costa, 1986).

Geomorphic effects of the dam- failure flood are locally conspicuous but highly variable. For example, channels for several miles (kilometers) below the Lawn Lake dam were widened tens of feet (meters) and scoured from 5 to 50 feet (1.5 to 15 m). An alluvial fan was deposited at the confluence of the Roaring River. The alluvial fan dammed the Fall River, forming a lake of 17 acres (6.9 ha) upstream from the fan (Jarrett and Costa, 1986). Few geomorphic changes occurred in the reach of the Fall River through Horseshoe Park because the gradient is very low, banks are well vegetated, and the floodwaters spread out over the entire valley floor (Pitlick, 1993b).

Studies concluded that the complex history of erosion and deposition in this gravel- bed river illustrate that floods in small drainage basins may produce highly variable geomorphic responses (Pitlick, 1993a).

Hydrogeology
The Continental Divide forms a mountain chain that runs the length of the park north- to- south and divides the park hydrologically. Waters on the park's west side form the headwaters of the Colorado River. East side streams and rivers are part of the Mississippi drainage.

Precambrian crystalline rocks underlie 95% of Rocky Mountain National Park. The Precambrian rocks (granite, gneiss, and schist) may contain small amounts of water in their fractures. The crystalline rocks are relatively impermeable and are generally poor aquifers. Wells intercepting fractures and weathered zones in these rocks commonly yield as many as 5 to 10 gallons (19 to 38 L) per minute from wells 100 to 200 feet (30 to 60 m) deep. Greater yields may be possible where several fracture sets intersect (Larry Martin, written communication, 2002).

Unconsolidated sedimentary deposits of Quaternary age underlie the large valleys in the park. These deposits, transported and deposited by glaciers and streams, may contain water in sand and gravel. The deposits contain sediments that range in size from clay to boulders and are generally poorly sorted. The deposits may be classified in two categories: moraines and outwash. Moraines generally form conspicuous ridges that border or terminate in flat- lying meadows. Because the moraines generally contain large amounts of clay and silt, and are poorly sorted, they yield only small amounts of water to wells (Larry Martin, written communication, 2002).

Glacial outwash and alluvial deposits, consisting of sand, silt, and gravel, underlie large parks, such as Moraine Park and Horseshoe Park. Streams have reworked outwash sediments, generally resulting in a sedimentary deposit that has had most of the clay removed and carried downstream. Wells constructed in outwash deposits can be very productive, yielding several hundred gallons (more than 1,000 L) per minute (Larry Martin, written communication, 2002).

Water Quality

Although quality is high in the park's waters as compared to much of the country, threats do exist. Nitrogen deposition is a factor influencing waters and soils in the park. In lakes and streams, the impacts of nitrogen deposition grow worse over time as the natural buffering capability of the soil and rock is used up. Eventually, chronic acidification can lead to the loss of many aquatic organisms and entire fish populations (Rocky Mountain National Park).

Surficial materials in the watersheds of Rocky Mountain National Park play a dominant role in evaluating sensitivity to acidification. Most soils in the area have formed from parent material of glacial or alluvial origin. The mineralogic composition of soils and overburden reflects parent rock type composition, susceptibility to chemical weathering, and climate. Investigators have determined that the rock types in the area (biotite gneiss, schist, and granite) have a statistically insignificant influence on the buffering capacity of soil tested. This resulted primarily from the low clay content of the soils which in turn was dependent on composition of parent rock type, rock weathering characteristics, and climate influence on rate and degree of weathering. Mineralogically, clay content is directly proportional to the buffering capacity of a soil. In the absence of clay, most of the buffering capacity of soils is attributed to decomposed organic matter and soil pH (Johnson and Herzog, 1982).
Landform types are useful in estimating the buffering capacity of surficial materials as they imply the amount of organic matter and the thickness of soil present. Examples of two landform types implying minimum and maximum capacities are bare bedrock and wet meadows. Thus the bedrock geology of the area is an important factor influencing water chemistry, while not significantly influencing the buffering capacity of the soils (Johnson and Herzog, 1982).

Wetlands

Wetlands are areas of high biological productivity and diversity and provide important sites for wildlife habitat. They serve as flood buffers and as filters, sequestering and storing heavy metals and other pollutants. By storing organic carbon in waterlogged sediments, wetlands also act as sinks for carbon. They are also sources of carbon, releasing carbon via degassing during decay processes, or after drainage and cutting, as a result of oxidation or burning. Wetlands develop naturally in response to morphological and hydrological features of the landscape. External factors such as climate change, landscape processes, or human activities can affect their evolution.

The meadows at the bottom of the Cache la Poudre Valley, with headwaters north of Fall River Pass, contain some of the park's major wetlands. Springs flowing into the valley from both sides keep the ground so saturated with water that trees cannot grow (Raup, 1996).

Diverting surface- water flow through the Grand Ditch has impacted wetlands, as well as groundwater level and spring activity, in the Kawuneeche Valley (Cooper and others, 2000). The impacts to wetlands include: (1) inhibiting geomorphic processes (e.g., frequency of flooding and channel- forming flows), (2) increasing exotic plant species, and (3) causing peatlands to lose carbon (Cooper and others, 2000).

Mass Wasting

Landslides

The landslides that have occurred in the park are Holocene and late Pleistocene in age (Braddock and Cole, 1990). Investigators have not determined the cause and frequency of landslides but have prepared a preliminary map of landslide deposits (Colton and others, 1975). This map, however, is not a substitute for careful detailed large- scale site investigations by engineering geologists and soil engineers (Colton and others, 1975). Park managers should conduct careful studies of areas susceptible to landslide and related activity before any development begins.

Landslides in the park include slumps and earth flows of glacial till along the sides of Kawuneeche Valley; large, nearly intact masses of volcanic rocks between Iron Mountain and Bald Mountain; and jumbled, hummocky masses of relatively intact blocks of Precambrian rocks (Braddock and Cole, 1990). Several areas of hummocky steps around Iceberg Lake are landslide deposits that slid down the steep slopes of the cirque (Raup, 1996).

A major landslide area on the flanks of Jackstraw Mountain can be seen across the tributary valley to the east of Farview Curve. The large slide on Jackstraw Mountain is composed of biotite schist. The foliation (compositional layering) in the schist around the slide area dips to the north and northwest, nearly parallel to the direction of slide movement (Bradock and Cole, 1990). The jumbled blocks in this landslide started moving after the tributary glacier in this valley melted between 15,000 and 12,000 years ago (Raup, 1996).

Debris Flows

On June 16, 1978, a mudflow deposited a lobate mass of mud, sand, and gravel on the west side of Kawuneeche Valley north of Baker Gulch. The so- called "Holzwarth debris flow" was initiated at an altitude of about 10,200 feet (3,110 m) when about 110 cubic yards (85 m³) of water- saturated debris occupying an area of about 300 square feet (2,790 dm³) suddenly began to slide. The sliding mass accelerated, incorporated more saturated debris, liquefied, and flowed to the base of the slope within a few minutes. The track of the debris flow varies from about 40 to 100 feet (12 to 30 m) wide. Within the track all the trees were removed, and in places a foot (30 cm) of soil was scoured away. Trees were pushed to the edge of the track and piled into a windrow of debris.

Surface flow of water down the track produced deep gullies. Tracks of a similar debris flow, which occurred between 1969 and 1974, are also present in Baker Gulch (Braddock and Cole, 1990).

Investigators suspect that the cause of this debris flow may be linked to changes in water flow in the Grand Ditch. Investigators have not performed a conclusive study, however.

Rockfalls

Talus deposits are present at the base of all steep slopes in the park. Talus slopes form as angular blocks of rock and abundant interstitial smaller rock fragments both on steep slopes and at the base of cliffs (Braddock and Cole, 1990). Researchers suggest that freeze- thaw processes cause rockfalls, which are also triggered by intense summer rainstorms (Caine, 1986). Rockfalls are the primary agents in the formation of talus, though some talus deposits were transported by debris flows and snow avalanches (Braddock and Cole, 1990). Most talus is Holocene in age (Braddock and Cole, 1990).

In a 20- year period at least three rockfalls involving more than 6.5 cubic yards (5.0 m³) of debris occurred in the upper Green Lakes valley in the Indian Peaks Wilderness south of the park. This study area is typical of high elevation environments on the east side of the Front Range [and in the park] (Caine, 1986). Each rockfall included clasts larger than 3 feet (nearly 1 m) that traversed the entire talus slope. In total they involved more than 200 cubic yards (150 m³) of rock (Caine, 1986). The movement within talus slopes themselves is generally about an inch (25 mm) per year in the Green Lakes area (Caine, 1986).

Investigators analyzed data during this study, which suggest that intervals of more active sediment production and transport have occurred since deglaciation of the alpine valleys at the end of the Pinedale glaciation (Caine, 1986). More active sediment production and transport in the past accounts for the present volumes of talus in today's alpine landscapes.

Although rockfalls are not as active as they once were, they do occur. Hence, because of their areal extent, rockfalls are significant for planning and public safety. Park managers should include talus slopes in the park's GIS because these data would be useful for planning or rerouting trails that cut across or below these slopes.

Minerals and Mining

Colorado Mineral Belt

Rocky Mountain National Park lies just north of the Colorado Mineral Belt—an area that contains most of the mining districts in Colorado. The mineral belt is 10–15 miles (16–24 km) wide and spans diagonally southwestward across the mountain ranges of Colorado from Jamestown in the Front Range to the San Juan Mountains in the southwestern part of the state. Igneous rocks of Laramide and younger ages and ore deposits of various types characterize the mineral belt (Pearson, 1980). Its northwest boundary is generally drawn to include mineralized areas and the Laramide stocks of the eastern part of the Indian Peaks Wilderness, just south of the park (Pearson, 1980).

The Jamestown, Ward, Gold Hill, and Caribou mining areas in the Boulder County tungsten district lie in the mineral belt within 6 miles (10 km) of the park. In addition, about 15 miles (24 km) south of the Indian Peaks Wilderness are the large disseminated molybdenum ore bodies at Urad and Henderson, and the base and precious metal veins in the Central City–Blackhawk district. Geologists also consider the minor Lost Lake and Lake Albion districts, partly in the Indian Peaks, to be part of the Colorado Mineral Belt (Pearson, 1980), as defined by the presence of Laramide intrusive bodies.

Except for the Urad and Henderson districts, Front Range mineral deposits typically occur as veins that occupy faults of small displacement—largely of Precambrian rocks but partly in Laramide intrusive rocks. Most of the faults are only a few hundred feet (meters) long, and few exceed 1 mile (1.6 km). Tweto (1968) summarized the Laramide- age ore bodies in these and other districts in the mineral belt of the Front Range.

> The ore deposits in such veins [those in Precambrian rocks] are in ore shoots that have thicknesses of several inches to a few feet, stope lengths of a few tens to a few hundreds of feet, and pitch lengths from a few tens to 1,000 feet. The ore bodies thus are small in tonnage, and many of them could be worked only because of their rather high grade, which in many cases was 1 to 10 ounces of gold or 50 to 500 ounces of silver per ton. Since the veins are discontinuous and the ore bodies are small, the outlook for future production from deposits of this kind is poor, primarily because the cost of discovery is high in proportion to the value of an ore body.

Although exploration and mining activity continue sporadically, particularly during periods of relatively high metal prices, the outlook for mining these veins in the Front Range is still pessimistic (Pearson, 1980). A proposed southern extension of the park—54 square miles (140 km²) of rugged mountain country to the east of Monarch Lake—would have included a portion of the now- Indian Peak Wilderness as part of the national park (Lovering and Goddard, 1938). Regarding the proposed southern extension of the park, investigators determined "mineral deposits throughout the area are not abundant" and "no deposits in the district are of commercial grade" (Lovering and Goddard, 1938).

Minerals

Pegmatites (see also Rock Units and Properties section of this report) and other sources of mineral specimens occur throughout the park, although not at commercial grades. However, these deposits may attract mineral collectors. For example, Specimen Mountain, once thought to be a volcano, is a pile of volcanic rock that accumulated during the same series of eruptions that deposited the rocks at Lava Cliffs (Raup, 1996). Specimen Mountain lives up to its name: samples found there are said to be "suitable for cutting" (Seaman, 1934). Locally the jasper forms geodes, partially or completely filled with agate, onyx, opal, calcite, and minor amounts of allophane and chloropal (Wahlstrom, 1941). Frank Byers, son of William Byers who climbed Longs Peak with John Wesley Powell in 1868, remembered that when he was a boy at his father's ranch in Hot Sulphur Springs, Specimen Mountain was called Geode Mountain (Arps and others, 1977).

Mining History

Most of the mining in the vicinity of Rocky Mountain National Park occurred outside the present- day boundary, but small workings at Eugenia Mine (on Battle Mountain near the Longs Peak Trail), North Star "Shipler" Mine (along the Colorado River Trail), and Prospect Canyon (in Glacier Gorge) attest to early prospecting and mining activity. Probably the most well-known mining area in the park is Lulu City, in Kawuneeche Valley. In 1879 a small party of prospectors out of Ft. Collins discovered silver along the North Fork of the Grand River (now the Colorado River) and located several mines, two of which were the North Star and Iron Mines in Kawuneeche Valley. Hearing of the discoveries, prospectors flocked to the area in pursuit of quick riches. By 1880 Lulu City was "home" to as many as 500 miners and had a butcher shop, a post office, a real estate agency, about 20 houses, and several mining companies. However, the riches did not materialize as fast as the town. By 1884 miners abandoned the town in search of other opportunities (U.S. Department of the Interior, National Park Service, Land Resources Division, Mining and Mineral Branch, 1993).

One miner, however, remained in the district until 1914, the year before the park was established. Joseph Shipler worked a small prospect on side of Shipler Mountain. He created a sizeable pile of mine waste and gathered a little silver ore (Kaye, 1983).

Colorado's mining history is full of scams, and Rocky Mountain National Park can boast of a scam as well. The Triumph Mine, part of the Lulu City district, was part of a mining scandal. The tailings were reportedly salted with high- grade ore from silver mines in Georgetown. Unwitting investors bought the claims but ended up owning nothing of economic value (Robert Higgins, National Park Service, Geologic Resources Division, Mining and Mineral Branch, memorandum, February 28, 1991).

Abandoned Mine Lands

In 1988, resource managers in Rocky Mountain National Park requested assistance from the NPS Mining and Minerals Branch to conduct an inventory and field inspections of abandoned mine lands (AML) in the park (RMP database, project number #ROMON550000). Staff

from the Mining and Minerals Branch assisted park resource managers with inventorying abandoned mine lands in the park. Staff identified and inventoried four AML sites: Meeker Park, Eugenia Mine (off the Longs Peak Trail), Miner Bill's Mine (Mount Chapin), North Star "Shipler" Mine (Lulu City area), and Aspen Brook site (Lily Lake area). Staff identified more than 20 mine openings (adits), with some posing moderate safety hazards.

After staff completed the inventory in 1993, park managers implemented mitigation at several sites. They sealed the Iron Mine and an unnamed mine next to the Iron Mine with rock and mortar. Managers closed the North Star "Shipler" Mine, along the Colorado River Trail, to human entry using a gate that still allows bats to enter and exit. The objective of the mitigation was to prevent park visitors from entering the mines, and potentially endangering themselves, while preserving the historic integrity of the area (U.S. Department of the Interior, National Park Service, Land Resources Division, Mining and Minerals Branch, 1993).

Seismicity

The Uniform Building Code Seismic Map (1979) designates Rocky Mountain National Park as a zone of minor seismic hazard, similar to most Colorado mountain areas. Since earliest records beginning in 1867, historical earthquake activity has affected the park. The largest historical earthquake in Colorado occurred on November 7, 1882, in the vicinity of Estes Park. This earthquake predates seismographs, so an estimated magnitude of 6.5 is based on the size of the area over which the earthquake was felt (Colorado Geological Survey, unpublished data, 1999). A large earthquake near the park could cause rockfalls and landslides, and changes in springs and streamflow (Geoindicators report, unpublished data, 2001).

Geologists have divided Colorado into seven seismotectonic provinces and estimated maximum credible earthquakes (MCE) for each province (Kirkham and Rogers, 1981). This subdivision places the park in the area called Eastern Mountain Province for which the estimated MCE is in the range of magnitude 6.0 to 6.75 on the Richter scale. In addition to seismic provinces, engineers include significant faults in seismotectonic evaluations: Laramie River, Frontal (Blue River), and Derby (U.S. Department of the Interior, Bureau of Reclamation, Division of Dam and Structural Safety, 1982). The Laramie River and the Frontal (Blue River) faults have MCE values of 7.0; the Derby fault has MCE of 6.25 (U.S. Department of the Interior, Bureau of Reclamation, Division of Dam and Structural Safety, 1982).

The Lawn Lake flood provided the impetus to remove four of the park's dams at high reservoirs: Lawn, Sandbeach, Pear, and Bluebird lakes. Lily and Sprague lakes have reservoirs (and dams) remaining. Although earthen dams are generally very stable in earthquakes (Jim Cole, written communication, 2003), determining the volumes of these remaining reservoirs and preparing an inundation map—including downstream hazards for camping and picnic areas—may provide valuable information for park planning and mitigation in the event of seismic activity and dam failure.

Water Diversion Projects

By the time Congress passed the bill that established Rocky Mountain National Park, 19 reservoirs and three water diversion projects had been approved within its boundaries for power and irrigation to the towns of Boulder, Longmont, and Loveland, among others. In all, more water developments were proposed or executed within today's park boundaries, than in all other national parks combined (U.S. Department of the Interior, National Park Service, Division of Interpretive Planning, Harpers Ferry Center, 1985).

Colorado–Big Thompson Project

The most ambitious trans- mountain water project to exist within the park is the Colorado–Big Thompson Project, which began in 1938 and was completed in the 1959 (Merriman, 1960). An important feature of this project is the 13.1- mile- long Alva B. Adams tunnel, which carries water underneath Rocky Mountain National Park from the wetter west side to the drier east side. The principal engineering structures of the entire project include: 13 reservoirs, 23 dams and [water] dikes, six power plants, 36 substations and seven switchyards, three pumping plants, 19 tunnels (34 mi, 55 km), more than 100 miles (160 km) of supply and feeder canals, and 785 miles (1,263 km) of transmission lines (Merriman, 1960).

Grand Ditch

Even at its headwaters, water from the tributaries to the Colorado River is diverted for use on the east side of the Continental Divide. The Grand Ditch transports water from the west side of the Continental Divide to the east side, across 13 miles (21 km) of the east slope of the Never Summer Mountains. The Grand River Ditch Company owns the Grand Ditch. The company established senior water rights prior to congressional designation of Rocky Mountain National Park. In 1894 the Water Supply and Storage Company began construction of an irrigation ditch about 1,000 feet (305 m) above the then- Grand River valley. According to the park's Web site, by 1934 water was flowing to farmers on the eastern plains (Rocky Mountain National Park). The Grand Ditch intercepts approximately one- third of the surface water runoff from the east side of the Never Summer Mountains. Research indicates that this disruption in the hydrology affects plant and animal life in the Kawuneeche Valley (Cooper and others, 2000). Because of the importance of the ditch to farmers and communities on the northern Colorado plains, park managers have not acquired additional water rights.

Hidden Valley

On a smaller scale than both the Colorado–Big Thompson Project and the Grand Ditch is the diversion of the stream in Hidden Valley. Workers buried the stream channel and installed culverts during construction of the Hidden Valley Ski Area. The ski area opened for business in 1952, although winter recreationists had used the area since the 1920s. A ski lift was installed in 1971. The ski area was closed permanently in 1992. For decades, the entire streamflow in the small watershed was diverted for making artificial snow. Park managers are in the process of restoring the stream channel and natural flow (Geoindicators report, unpublished data, 2001).

Removal of Dams

The Lawn Lake flood provided the impetus to remove four of the park's high mountain reservoirs in the park. After acquiring the water rights, park managers removed what remained of the earthen dam at Lawn Lake, some 5,300 cubic yards (4,050 m³) or 450 [vertical] feet (140 m) of earthen embankment (Rocky Mountain National Park).

Park managers have removed three other high mountain dams. In 1988 they removed rock and dirt dams at Sandbeach Lake and Pear Lake, and then regraded the land to the original slope. In 1989 and 1990 they removed five million pounds (2,268,000 kg) of concrete and rebar from the Bluebird Lake dam. Park managers recycled the materials near Lily Lake. About 67 acres (27 ha) of shoreline around all three lakes were reexposed, and park managers are currently allowing the shores to restore naturally (Rocky Mountain National Park).

Remaining Reservoirs

Rocky Mountain National Park has two remaining water reservoirs: Lily Lake and Sprague Lake. Each of these lakes supports recreational fishing activity and hosts handicap accessible fishing areas. Park managers have no plans to remove the impoundment structures at these popular areas.

Wind-Blown Sediment

Wind- blown detritus is the dominant sediment source for alpine lakes in Colorado (Caine, 1974). Aeolian dust is transported through alpine hillslope systems and is stored in alpine lakes and tundra soils (Caine, 1986). In the context of the park's close proximity to metropolitan areas of the Front Range, this information is significant with respect to incoming pollutants.

Cumulative evidence from multiple studies in Rocky Mountain National Park (Loch Vale) and adjacent areas along the Colorado Front Range (Niwot Ridge) strongly suggest that present levels of nitrogen deposition are currently altering terrestrial and aquatic ecosystems on the eastern side of the mountains (Rocky Mountain National Park). Hence, the information provided in this report may simply be putting a geologic spin on an already- identified concern. Nevertheless, park managers are encouraged to study the wind- blown sediment in alpine systems and identify sources of the sediment. Furthermore, park managers are encouraged to include aeolian processes in the park's inventory and monitoring program. The information gained from this study may assist with future management decisions, as well as setting air- quality standards in the Front Range.

Potential Research, Inventory, and Monitoring Projects

This information addresses the desire of park managers to identify relevant geologic research projects (Terry Terrell, oral communication, 2002). It also highlights the range of possibilities for research in the park, the use of data for interpretive purposes, and the importance of identifying resources in order to protect them. The list is not prioritized.

Geologic research is useful for gaining information and understanding of natural resources beyond what is typically thought of as geology. For example, assistance with the identification of already- mapped rhyolite exposures on the west side of the park would help pinpoint the locations for certain rare mosses that exist in the park and need to be protected. Also, dryas, an alpine flower that grows on limestone in Europe, grows in tundra areas of the park, which are not underlain by limestone. Analyzing the sources of soil components and geomorphic processes that allow this rare plant to unexpectedly grow in the park would aid in understanding the alpine tundra environment.

Research in Rocky Mountain National Park can have international significance. For example, at a site in Loch Vale, near Sky Pond, investigators linked a glacial deposit with the European Younger Dryas (interval of late-glacial time about 10,500 years ago). This Santanta Peak moraine was deposited at the end of the Pleistocene ice age. The Satanta Peak advance began between 11,000 and 12,000 years ago and ended about 10,000 years ago. This finding is important because understanding the worldwide extent, timing, and relative magnitude of the Younger Dryas event is scientifically significant for understanding the mechanism responsible for abrupt climate change (Menounos and Reasoner, 1997).

Determine extent of landslide hazards in the park

Staff at the U.S. Geological Survey (USGS) proposed that the western part of Rocky Mountain National Park be a study site for a project entitled "Landslide recurrence and slope evolution in the western United States" (1993–1997). Because of retiring personnel, this particular project ended before any work was done in the park. Later, other USGS personnel initiated and executed a study at one of the proposed sites—the Interstate 70 corridor.

Nevertheless, work on the western slope in the park is still significant. For example, the upper parts of the Colorado and Laramie Rivers, including the beheaded part of the Laramie River now known as Joe Wright Creek, are in a fault zone that contains weak rocks of Mesozoic and Cenozoic ages that are susceptible to landslides. A large landslide beheaded the Laramie River and dammed the valley at what is now the upvalley end of Chambers Lake. Water impounded by this landslide eventually cut an outlet that allowed the lake to drain into the Cache la Poudre River (Rich Madole, written communication, 1998).

Without further study, investigators cannot assess the extent of slope- failure risk to the park's infrastructure. The risk does not appear to be great on the east slope of the Front Range, but some does exist (Rich Madole, written communication, 1998). Specific aspects of landslides to be studied are: (1) susceptibility of Tertiary volcanic rocks to landslides and (2) relationship between metamorphic foliation and landslide potential (Jim Cole, written communication, 1998).

Determine potential for debris flows below the Grand Ditch

The Holzwarth debris flow was deposited on June 16, 1978, on the west side of Kawuneeche Valley north of Baker Gulch. Tracks of a similar debris flow, which occurred between 1969 and 1974, are also present in Baker Gulch (Braddock and Cole, 1990). Investigators suspect that the debris flows in this area are linked to diversion of water into the Grand Ditch but do not have conclusive information regarding the cause or the potential for future debris- flow events.

Study early history of Colorado (Grand) River drainage

The field area would consist of the landscape preserved below the Never Summer–Specimen Mountain volcanics. The study would look at the relationship between the Troublesome Formation and the paleogeography of the upper Colorado River drainage.

Conduct a detailed study of high-grade metamorphic rocks

Many aspects of metamorphic rocks in and surrounding the park are not well understood. Examples of potential research projects include: (1) the chemical reactions involved in partial melting of the metamorphic rocks, (2) geochemical changes in mineral compositions, (3) pressure- temperature- time relations between the low-grade rocks in the lower Big Thompson canyon and the zone of melting, and (4) origin and significance of retrograde minerals in the metamorphic rocks (e.g., muscovite, tourmaline, and topaz).

Examine Troublesome Formation for paleontological resources

The park is not known for its paleontological resources however, one unit is of interest with respect to fossils. Most of the rocks in the park are Precambrian gneisses and schists, with some volcanic rocks of Tertiary age. The Troublesome Formation—sedimentary rock of early Miocene and late Oligocene time in the vicinity of the park, primarily Middle Park, has yielded various fossil mammals (Lovering, 1930; Izett, 1974), such as rodents similar to pocket gophers (Lewis, 1969; Kron, 1988). Outcrops of the Troublesome Formation on the west side of the park are probably fossiliferous (Casey McKinney, written communication, 2003).

Determine geomorphic history of Black Canyon drainage

Glacial processes are expected to have played a role in the development of the Black Canyon drainage in the northeast portion of the park. However, evidence of glacial activity is not readily apparent (Jim Cole, written communication, 1998). This puzzle has long intrigued geologists working in the area.

Determine the origin of the flat lands in Estes Park

Understanding the origin of the flat lands in Estes Park is significant for interpreting the evolution of the area's landscape and the drainage on the east side of Rocky Mountain National Park (Jim Cole, written communication, 1998).

Expand study of emplacement mechanisms of Longs Peak–St Vrain batholith

Researchers have not fully studied the area that hosts the Longs Peak–St. Vrain batholith (Jim Cole, written communication, 1998). A potential research project could include the area beyond that which was covered by Cole (1977).

Refine petrologic studies of granitic rocks of Silver Plume intrusive event

Researchers need to refine the origin and significance of unusual aluminous minerals (e.g., garnet, sillimanite) in some parts of the Silver Plume Granite. For example, a research project that quantifies the volatile content in the granite magmas and late-stage evolution of volatile (gas) phase and brecciation needs to be completed.

Clarify geologic details of Never Summer Mountains

Researchers have not studied in detail the timing and kinematics of the Never Summer thrust or the emplacement and subsequent deformation by the Never Summer intrusions (Jim Cole, written communication, 1998). Research would provide important information about the Cenozoic depositional and tectonic history of the park.

Monitor mass balance of glaciers

Investigators do not know whether the masses of ice in the park are shrinking or growing over long periods of time (Braddock and Cole, 1990). Knowledge of seasonal mass balances (e.g., summer and winter) would shed light on glacier fluctuations in the park. For example, it would help answer questions such as: is glacier contraction caused primarily by less nourishment in winter or by more melt in summer? Monitoring of mass balance would also assist in the interpretation of streamflow records.

Data from the park's glaciers could be shared with the Global Terrestrial Network-Glacier (GTN-G) of World Meteorological Organization's (WMO) Global Climate Observing Network (GCOS). In addition, Rocky Mountain National Park could be part of the Global Terrestrial Observing Systems (GTOS), Terrestrial Monitoring System (TEMS).

Conduct comprehensive study of structural geology of the park

A comprehensive study of the structural geology specific to the park is needed. Such a study could include a map of faults and their maximum credible earthquake potentials, evidence for the park's structure fitting into the theory of plate tectonics, and data regarding the uplifted erosion surface in the park's high country (see "Uplifted Erosion Surface" in "Geologic Features and Processes"). Researchers could also study the relationship between regional uplift and climate change (e.g., cooling during glaciations). Such a study, and the accompanying manuscript, would be useful for resource managers and interpreters alike.

Promote the park as a laboratory for mountain geomorphology

Landforms and processes related to all four major geologic agents—the work of water, ice, mass movement (gravity), and wind—exist in the alpine environments within the park (Rich Madole, written communication, 1998). These landforms and processes further relate to studies of Pleistocene and Holocene deposits and sedimentary records of climate in ice-marginal and post-glacial settings (Jim Cole, written communication, 1998).

The recognition by park managers that Rocky Mountain National Park is a laboratory for mountain geomorphology can be used to their advantage. Advertising this fact to the scientific community would result in data and information that could be used in making management decisions regarding the park's natural resources, as well as in preparing interpretive materials and exhibits.

Gather information on regional alpine studies

Several agencies conducting regional alpine studies are located in the Front Range near Rocky Mountain National Park. These studies may provide local baseline data and long-term trends associated with glacial fluctuations and frozen-ground activity. Agencies and programs to consider the Niwot Ridge Long Term Ecological Research Program, monitoring programs in the Indian Peaks Wilderness (University of Colorado) and Loch Vale (U.S. Geological Survey), and research at the Institute for Alpine and Arctic Research (INSTAAR) in Boulder. These agencies and programs also can provide standardized techniques and established protocols for monitoring alpine processes.

Develop snow avalanche maps for visitor safety and environmental studies

For the reason of visitor safety, park managers should determine whether the Colorado Avalanche Information Center or INSTAAR have mapped snow-avalanche areas in the park.

In addition to visitor safety, snow avalanches are landscape disturbances that help shape ecosystems. Avalanche paths are generally productive environments and provide habitats that serve as migration paths for large mammals, fuel breaks for fire, and conduits for carbon and sediment from higher to lower elevations.

Determine former locations of tree line–tundra interface

The tree line–tundra interface is an important marker for understanding paleoclimates. Tree line position may be a better indicator of climate change than monitoring glacier fluctuations in the park. A possible study is to determine the location of the former tree line–tundra ecotone and evaluate what controls its position.

Determine the depth and thickness of the permafrost and monitor the rate of creep

Knowing rates of creep would be useful for park planning and to the park's maintenance staff. Staff could be trained to use frost tubes to monitor rates of movement, which can be calibrated with monitoring studies at INSTAAR.

Monitor dust deposition in the park

The U.S. Geological Survey has developed standardized protocols for monitoring dust deposition. Park managers could incorporate dust monitoring into the existing air-quality monitoring program, thereby quantifying the dust component of the airborne particulate matter and identifying source areas of the particulate matter. This data will help determine whether there is a relationship between dust deposition and nitrate concentrations.

Establish a lake-level monitoring program

Historical fluctuations in lake levels provide a detailed record of climate changes on a scale of 10 years to 1 million years. Lakes are dynamic systems that are sensitive to local climate and to land- use changes in the surrounding landscape. Some lakes receive their water mainly from precipitation, some are dominated by rainfall and snowmelt runoff from drainage networks, and others are controlled by groundwater systems. The areal extent and depth of water in lakes are indicators of changes in climatic parameters such as precipitation, radiation, temperature, and wind speed. Where not directly affected by human actions, lake level fluctuations are excellent indicators of drought conditions. Lakes can also be valuable indicators of near- surface groundwater conditions.

In general, park staff could observe and record seasonal variability of lake levels. Park managers could also select particular lakes for more formal monitoring.

Monitor lake ice phrenology

Global climate change occurs naturally, but human activities can accelerate the process. Monitoring the first thaw–first freeze of lakes in the park provides an early warning of global warming. While park managers cannot directly address global warming issues through their management of park resources, knowing when impacts are occurring is useful. One approach would be to monitor ice phrenology, i.e., determine the date of first freeze and first thaw for alpine lakes; thereby, providing baseline data of long- term climate change.

Determine fire history, ecotones, and paleoclimate information from sediment cores

The chemical, physical, and biological character of aquatic sediments can provide a finely resolvable record of environmental change, in which natural events may be clearly distinguishable from human inputs. Information recorded in wetlands, lakes, and marshes would provide a perspective of fire history, ecotones, and paleoecology in the park. Investigators could obtain and analyze sediment cores from selected lakes, marshes, and wetlands in the park.

Develop strategies for restoration and monitoring of stream and wetlands at Hidden Valley

Park managers should consult personnel in the NPS Water Resources Division regarding restoration strategies of the stream and wetland at Hidden Valley. Replicating channel gradient and channel dimension is more important than the exact location of the original stream. The Water Resources Division could also assist in developing a monitoring program to quantify the response of the stream channel and wetlands restoration.

Monitor channel changes in response to removal of check dams

Park managers have inventoried 210 check dams in the park, and the park has an active program of removing old or failed check dams. Removal of check dams will alter streamflow and sediment transport and may change channel morphology downstream. The channels downstream should be monitored, including quantifying channel changes and stream response to the removal of check dams on park streams.

Geologic Features and Processes

Rocky Mountain National Park abounds in geologic features that may be of concern for park planning, public safety, or resource protection. Geologic features (or landforms) and processes have scientific and aesthetic significance, as well as continually affecting human beings and other living things. These features and processes may not be readily apparent on the park's geologic map.

Colorado River

The Colorado River originates in Kawuneeche Valley in Rocky Mountain National Park. Here it is very narrow, contrasting greatly with the segment of the river that flows through Grand Canyon National Park. The river flows 1,400 miles (2,253 km) from its birthplace in the park to the Gulf of California.

Columnar Jointing

High above the floor on the east side of Kawuneeche Valley in the vicinity of the Bowen- Baker Trailhead, a lava flow of rhyolite displays a peculiar type of jointing. This ornate rock feature, called columnar jointing, is not caused by weathering or erosion but by contraction of molten rock as it cools. This process produces parallel, prismatic columns that are polygonal in cross section. The lava flowed from one of the volcanoes in the Never Summer Mountains about 26 million years ago (Raup, 1996). The position of the lava flow high above the valley floor indicates that this valley was filled to that level with volcanic ash and lava at the time of the eruption. Erosion by water and ice in the ensuing years has removed most of the volcanic rocks and cut the valley to its present level (Raup, 1996).

Exfoliation Domes and Ornate Erosion Features

The rounded knobs on McGregor Mountain and Lumpy Ridge are homogeneous masses of granite with very uniform structure. As erosion of overlying rocks—presumably thousands of feet of sedimentary rock—slowly released pressure from the granite, exfoliation domes were formed. The granite responded by expanding and cracking into concentric slabs that resemble the rings of an onion.

Fractures that form in response to the removal of overlying rock may be quite prominent, in which case they often result in "sheeting" and sometimes form bizarre landforms. Helped along by frost action, sheeting produced the Keyhole on the popular route to the summit of Longs Peak.

Over millions of years, wind erosion and freeze- thaw action have sculpted the rocks in the park into many ornate forms. On Lumpy Ridge, for example, fantastically shaped rocks include balanced rock and clusters of oddly shaped boulders, such as "hen and chicks."

Glacial Features

Cirques and Tarns

Few landforms have caught the imagination of geomorphologists more than the glacial cirque: a bowl- shaped, amphitheater- like hollow or basin eroded into a mountain mass. The small glaciers that exist in the park occupy cirques once excavated by their large predecessors. After the glacier that created the cirque melts, a small lake, called a tarn, may occupy the basin. One of the most spectacular cirques is the area below the East Face of Longs Peak. Chasm Lake (a tarn) fills the basin. Other distinctive cirques in the park are located on Terra Tomah and Ypsilon Mountains.

Glacial Erratics

In many glaciated areas, large boulders end up stranded when glaciers recede. These out- of- place rocks are called erratics. Erratics testify to the effectiveness of glacial erosion and transport, and may have glacial striations. They also testify to glacial deposition and lie scattered on bedrock surfaces different from their own compositions. Visitors can see nice examples of erratics along the Cub Lake trail.

Glacial Polish, Striations, and Grooves

Rocks and sediment frozen to the base and sides of glaciers act like sandpaper and grind, scratch, and polish the rocks over which they pass. Transported rocks also become smoothed and rounded themselves. Glacial polish, striations, and grooves line Old Fall River Road, which leads to the head of the glacial valley at Fall River Pass.

Glacial Till and Moraines

A glacier carries all sizes of debris at its base, sides, and surface, and deposits this material along the sides and floor of the valley down which it flows. Till is the general term for the poorly sorted mixture of fine to coarse rock debris deposited directly from glacier ice. The most obvious landforms composed of till are moraines. Moraines can be undulating mounds or sharp ridges depending on how long a glacier remained stable in a particular position or how much erosion and weathering have taken place in the intervening time between deposition and the present.

Lateral moraines form on the sides of glaciers and merge with an end or terminal moraine, an arc- like ridge that forms at the terminus of glaciers. Excellent examples of lateral moraines are on the north and south sides of Moraine Park. The south lateral moraine is nearly 1,000 feet (305 m) high. An end (terminal) moraine forms when ice stabilizes for a time prior to retreat. An end moraine may dam meltwater to create a lake on its upvalley side. Moraine Park Museum sits on an end moraine, which also happens to be the terminal moraine, and represents the furthest point of glacial advance. A good viewing point of moraines is Many Parks Curve.

Hanging Valleys

Few landscape features are aesthetically more beautiful than a hanging valley with a high cascade or waterfall. A hanging valley that is formed by glacial erosion (there are other kinds of hanging valleys) is a side valley with its mouth at a relatively high level above the main glacial valley; it is smaller than the main valley. A "trunk" glacier eroded the larger, main valley, and a tributary glacier eroded the smaller hanging valley. The discordance of the levels of the valley floors, as well as their difference in size, is due to the greater erosive power of the main, trunk glacier. Some lakes, such as Nanita and Nokoni, lie in hanging valleys. Streams that occupy hanging valleys are Roaring River, Chiquita Creek, and Fern Creek.

Horns, Arêtes, and Cols

Mountains that are, or have been, surrounded by glaciers tend to have characteristic forms caused by the fracturing action of ice, leading to steep rockwalls at the heads of cirques that flank peaks. Where isolated, such mountains may form upstanding horns with three or four distinct faces. The most famous horn is the Matterhorn in the Swiss Alps. The Little Matterhorn, tucked away in Glacier Gorge, is less spectacular than its Swiss namesake but it still possesses distinctly carved faces. Sometimes steep, straight ridges, called arêtes, may link horns and cols—open, U- shaped passes. A good example of a col lies above Andrews Glacier in Loch Vale. This particular col directs wind- blown snow, carried over the Continental Divide, onto the surface of this "wind drift" glacier.

Outwash Deposits, Kettles, and Kettle Ponds

During a warming trend as a glacier recedes, a stream laden with sediment is "washed out" from the glacier (hence the term "outwash") and deposited in a flat area below. In mountainous areas, these deposits are called valley trains. Depressions, known as kettles, often pockmark outwash and moraines. Kettles form when a block of stagnant ice becomes wholly or partially buried in sediment and ultimately melts, leaving a pit behind. Kettles can be feet or miles long but are usually shallow. In many cases, water eventually fills the depression and forms a pond or lake, called a kettle pond or kettle lake. Sheep Lakes are kettle ponds that lie in the outwash on the floor of Horseshoe Park. These small ponds are intermittent and usually dry up late in the summer. Bighorn sheep visit these kettle ponds, primarily during their lambing season in May and June, to drink the water

and eat the mud, which is rich in nutrients for lactating ewes. We have the glaciers to thank for this prime wildlife- viewing area.

Roches Moutonnées

Roches moutonnées are characteristic of glacial erosion on massive rocks. Roches moutonnées are asymmetrical, elongate knobs or hillocks of resilient bedrock that have been smoothed and scoured by moving ice on the upglacier (stoss) side. On the down (lee) side, the rock is steep and hackly from glacial quarrying. Moutonnées are the wigs—with smooth bangs and curly backs—that barristers and judges wore in early European and British courts and resemble this glacial form. People have also interpreted roches moutonnées as "rock sheep," as they are thought to resemble grazing sheep. The knob in the middle of Moraine Park is a fair example of a roche moutonnée.

U-shaped Valleys

Prior to the appearance of glaciers, alpine valleys are characteristically V- shaped, as is typical for valleys cut by streams. As a glacier moves down a valley, it makes the valley wider, steeper, and straighter, so that the previous V- shaped valley is transformed into a U- shaped one. Good examples of U- shaped valleys are abundant in the park, for instance, the valley of Fall River and Kawuneeche Valley. When glaciers retreat, the bottoms of U- shaped valleys may become flat, as sediment deposited in lakes impounded by the terminal moraines fills them.

Glaciers

Today, the park's small glaciers are restricted to high elevations above 11,000 feet (3,350 m) and north- and east- facing cirques, where they are sheltered from the Sun's direct rays. Local topography helps to shelter the glaciers and directs wind- blown snow onto their surfaces. In general, during the winter blowing snow occurs over 50% of the time, with 95% of the days in January having blowing snow. On average, over 30 blowing snow events occur each winter, with each event averaging 36- hours long (Berg, 1986). Hence, glaciers in the Front Range are referred to as "wind- drift glaciers" because they receive most of their snow as wind- blown snow, which falls predominantly on the western slope and is transported to the eastern slope. Notably, these glaciers have been able to form well below regional snowline because of wind drift. A fine example of a wind- drift glacier in the park is Andrews Glacier.

Braddock and Cole (1990) identified 34 snow banks and ice masses in the vicinity of Rocky Mountain National Park. These include the snow and ice bodies shown on 1:24,000- scale topographic maps published between 1957 and 1962. Fourteen of the ice masses have been named: Rowe Glacier (between Rowe Peak and Hagues Peak), Sprague Glacier (at Irene Lake in Spruce Canyon), Tyndall Glacier (at the head of Tyndall Creek), Andrews Glacier (east of Andrews Pass), Taylor Glacier (at the head of Icy Brook), Chiefs Head Peak Glacier (above Frozen Lake), Mills Glacier (on the east side of Longs

Peak), Moomaw Glacier (south of The Cleaver), and the six St. Vrain Glaciers (outside of the park at the head of Middle St. Vrain Creek).

All but one of these snow banks or ice masses are on the east side of the Continental Divide; the exception is the mass above Murphy Lake (near Snowdrift Peak). All but one occur at the heads of cirques: north- , northeast- , or east- facing; the exception is the large snowbank northeast of Rowe Mountain, which is in a northeast-facing gully. Some of the ice masses, such as Andrews Glacier, are actively moving and can be considered actual glaciers; others are stagnant. Over long periods of time, it is not known whether these masses are growing or shrinking (Braddock and Cole, 1990).

Rock Glaciers

Rock glaciers are distinctive from ice glaciers in that their movement is characterized by a large amount of embedded and overlying rock material. A rock glacier may be composed of (1) ice- cemented rock formed in talus that is subject to permafrost, (2) ice- cemented rock debris formed from avalanching snow and rock, or (3) rock debris that has a core of ice, either a debris- covered glacier or a remnant moraine. Two types of rock glaciers occur in the Front Range. The first type forms on the floors of modern cirques and closely resembles the tongues of small valley glaciers. They are referred to as cirque- floor rock glaciers (Outcalt and Benedict, 1965) or tongue- shaped rock glaciers (Madole, 1972). Because they contain cores of banded glacial ice and grade upvalley into lateral moraines, investigators determine rock glaciers of this type to represent the debris- covered tongues of former glaciers in the Front Range. This may not be true everywhere, however (Madole, 1972). Most cirque- floor rock glaciers consist of two or more superimposed lobes, bounded by longitudinal furrows, resulting from independent ice advances. Despite their compound nature, the complexes now appear to be moving downslope as single units (Outcalt and Benedict, 1965).

Rock glaciers of an entirely different character occur beneath steep valley walls, where they are supplied with debris from avalanche couloirs. Interstitial ice, responsible for the movement of the "valley- wall" rock glaciers, probably results from the metamorphism of snow buried beneath rockfall debris or supplied by winter avalanching (Outcalt and Benedict, 1965). Geologists also refer to this type of rock glacier as a lobate- shaped rock glacier (Madole, 1972).

In Rocky Mountain National Park, rock glaciers either accumulate at heads of cirques and flow down the length of the main valley or accumulate along the sides of valleys and flow outward toward the center. Rock glaciers are abundant on both sides of the Continental Divide and both sides of the Never Summer Mountains, and have flowed down slopes that face all compass directions (Braddock and Cole, 1990). Rock glaciers occur on Ships Prow, Pagoda Mountain, and Storm Peak on the east side of the park, and near Azure, Julian, and Hayden lakes on the west side of the park (Braddock and Cole, 1990).

Lakes

Numerous lakes—nearly 150—punctuate the landscape of Rocky Mountain National Park. They come in many shapes and sizes, and their origins vary.

As the large valley glaciers retreated, they left basins in their paths. Today, chains of glacial lakes are found in these deprressions and appear as treads of a rising staircase. The term paternoster, i.e., "Our Father," is an apt description for these chains of lakes, as they resemble the beads on a rosary. An example of paternoster lakes is the linked Fifth–Fourth–Spirit–Verna–Lone Pine lakes on the west side of the park. Some, such as Gorge Lakes (seen from Trail Ridge looking across Forest Canyon), fill glacially carved but do not form chains. Others, such as Forest Lake and Bierstadt Lake—additional examples of kettle ponds—formed behind dams of glacial moraine (Emerick, 1995).

A number of small pothole ponds, formed by weathering of exposed bedrock, lie among the granite outcrops along Lumpy Ridge. The largest of these is Gem Lake, a rain- fed pond with no inlet or outlet (Emerick, 1995).

Ponds and lakes are among the most temporary features of the landscape. Though they may seem long- lived in terms of human generations, lakes gradually fill with sediment and become shallower and smaller (Emerick, 1995).

Meandering Streams

Streams constantly erode their banks and deposit new sediment; hence, riparian zones change more than any other type of ecosystem in the park. In flat valleys, streams tend to meander, widening their bends and occasionally short- circuiting them, leaving the abandoned meanders to form oxbow lakes, which over time fill in with sediment. Floods that result from snowy winters and wet springs may scour channels or form new stream courses.

Meandering streams are typical of streams in the park because gradients are low behind the Pleistocene moraine dams. In many cases, meandering streams represent lake floors of past glacial lakes or outwash deposits. Good examples of meandering streams are in the area surrounding the Bowen- Baker Trailhead, where the Colorado River meanders across the valley, and Horseshoe Park. Horseshoe Park earned its name through this geomorphic process: loops in the meandering stream that have been cut off and left behind as isolated sections, resemble horseshoes.

Patterned Ground

Today the term periglacial is used to describe processes and landforms associated with very cold climates in areas not permanently covered with snow and ice. Periglacial features are distinctive from glacial features and in many cases are located far from glaciers. One particular periglacial features in Rocky Mountain National Park is patterned ground, which forms at high elevations, above about 11,500 feet (3,505 m) in the Front Range (Ives and Fahey, 1971). An interesting effect of ice-crystal growth in soils (ground ice) is the moving of soil and rock fragments upward toward the surface to form mounds and rows of soil or rock. Rock fragments lying close to the surface conduct heat causing a cycle of freezing and thawing and growth of ice under rocks. Continued thickening of ice layers heaves rocks upward, causing them to rise to the surface. Frost action moves rocks both sideways and upward. Heaved rocks form patterns of bands, circles, nets, and polygons called patterned ground.

Large angular blocks of rock in an accumulation known as felsenmeer (German for "rock sea") are a conspicuous display of frost action above treeline. People have also described them as "tombstone rocks" (Kiver and Harris, 1999). A popular stopping point along Trail Ridge Road is Rock Cut. Tundra Communities Trail leading from the road provides easy access through felsenmeer and patterned ground.

Sackung

Many geologic features do not fit nicely into just one category; sackung features are a case in point being both glacial and structural. As thick, mountain glaciers carved their way down preexisting valleys, they caused two changes: they steepened the valley walls, and to a lesser degree, they deepened the valleys. When the ice filled these valleys, the glaciers provided lateral support to the valley walls. When the ice melted, the steep valley walls lost their support. Gravity caused the mountains between the over-steepened valleys to actually spread laterally into the valleys. Small faults along the tops and sides of ridge crests were created that commonly have uphill-facing scarps called sackung features. In the past, geologists have thought these faults were caused by mountain-building processes; they now know they were caused by mountain "falling" processes.

Solifluction

The term solifluction was proposed by Andersson (1906) as "the slow flowing from higher to lower ground of masses of waste saturated with water." Because Andersson did not state explicitly that it referred to flow over frozen ground, some geomorphologists have extended the term to include similar movement in temperate and tropical regions. It is preferable to restrict the term to slow soil movement in periglacial areas, however (Bates and Jackson, 1987). (See also Geologic Issues section of this report.)

The term solifluction implies the presence of permafrost. Permafrost (i.e., permanently frozen ground) has no doubt existed over most of the alpine zone in the past, but it is discontinuous today (Rich Madole, written communication, 2003).

During the summer season in the high country, water is unable to percolate into an impervious layer of frozen ground below the surface. As a result an "active layer" of soil becomes supersaturated and flows. Flowage can occur on slopes as gentle as two or three degrees. Where there is a well-developed mat of vegetation, a sheet may move downward in a series of well-defined lobes and form terrace-like features. Features formed by soil flowage appear as wavy slopes and are quite prominent along Trail Ridge Road, for example, between Forest Canyon Overlook and Rock Cut.

Tors

Tors are isolated rock towers rising prominently above otherwise level terrain. They are typically composed of granite, which is very jointed and made more so by sheer jointing that develops because of dilation as rock is unloaded. Tors may assume peculiar or fantastic shapes. Visitors can see excellent examples along the nature walk above Rock Cut on Trail Ridge Road. Investigators think that periglacial processes may be important in the formation of tors (Bates and Jackson, 1987). Investigators have identified tors as indicators of non-glaciation (Street, 1973). Tors remain in areas that were beyond the limit of glaciation, otherwise glaciers would have modified or destroyed them.

Uplifted Erosion Surface

The so-called "Roof of the Rockies" is a remnant of an ancient rolling plain that has survived despite being broken by faults, uplifted several thousand feet, intersected by great canyons, and subjected to the vicissitudes of the Ice Age (Richmond, 1974). Big Horn Flats and the flat, plain-like surface that spans across the landscape between 11,000 and 12,000 feet (3,350 to 3,660 m) on Trail Ridge are parts of this uplifted erosion surface.

Since the erosion surface was first recognized and reported (Marvine, 1874), it has caught the attention of geologists and visitors alike, but not without controversy. Questions still remain regarding: (1) the number of surfaces—investigators have recognized as few as one to as many as 11 surfaces; (2) the age—early or late Tertiary, that is 5 million or 50 million years old; and (3) the genesis—peneplain (forming at low elevations and with low river gradients) vs. pediment (forming under arid conditions along mountain fronts or plateaus).

Geologists have paid so much attention to erosion surfaces because of the structural implications. For decades, geologists used erosion surfaces as a clue to the post-Laramide deformational history of the middle and southern Rocky Mountains. Because peneplains were believed to form at low elevations and with low river gradients, substantial uplift was required to bring them to their present elevations. Using this kind of evidence, investigators estimated late Cenozoic uplift to between 5,000 and 9,000 feet (1,524 and 2,743 m) (Davis, 1911; Chamberlain, 1919). Reclassifying peneplains as pediments greatly reduced the amount of uplift required (Johnson, 1931, 1932; Mackin, 1947). Uplift was then estimated from displaced flora and fauna, for example using fossils from Florissant, Colorado (Epis and Chapin,

1975). The curious irony is that the magnitude of uplift based on paleontology is approximately the same as it was when based on peneplains (Bradley, 1987).

The most recent theory regarding erosion surfaces identifies one major subsummit (lower) surface and a second (higher) summit surface. The lower surface formed in late Tertiary time when conditions were arid to semi- arid, classifying it as a pediment. The higher surface is much less extensive than the lower subsummit surface. Studies have concentrated on the lower erosion surface that has been called "Rocky Mountain," "Sherman," "Late Eocene," and "Subsummit," which leaves the full significance of the higher surface, which has been called "Flattop" and "Summit," inconclusive (Bradley, 1987). Terra Tomah Mountain, Flattop Mountain, and Longs Peak are all part of the higher summit surface.

Formation Properties

This section serves as the critical link between resource managers and the geologic map of the park. Formation Tables are highly generalized and for informational purposes only. Ground disturbing activities should not be permitted or denied on the basis of information contained in these tables. More detailed unit descriptions can be found in the help files accompanying the digital geologic map or by contacting the Geologic Resources Division at 303- 969- 2090.

This section provides readily available information about the rock units (deposits and formations—lithologically distinct, mappable bodies of rock) in Rocky Mountain National Park, including age, unit name, map symbol, locations within the park, description, local and global significance, geologic hazards within the unit, suitability for development and recreation, and resource potential and protection.

Not all the rock units identified on *Geologic Map of Rocky Mountain National Park and Vicinity, Colorado* (Braddock and Cole, 1990) are addressed. Only the rocks that occur within the park's boundary and illustrate significant geologic events or processes are listed. Rock units are organized from youngest to oldest.

Although none of the units contain mineral deposits of commercial values, many units contain specimens that may be temptations to casual collectors, and therefore, are notable for resource protection. Some of the units are mined for building stone and sand and gravel elsewhere.

In the table, found on the following pages, "Ma" represents "millions of years." In addition, although some of the units should be evaluated for flooding potential prior to development, intense mountain floods, on the scale of the Big Thompson Flood of 1976, are statistically unlikely above 8,000 feet (2,438 m).

Geologic History

Precambrian Time

Ancient rocks form the core of the mountains in Rocky Mountain National Park. These rocks are more than 1,700 million years old and are from Precambrian time. In areas less exposed to the forces of heat and pressure (and accompanying recrystallization of rocks) sedimentary features still exist and display original sedimentary structures, which aid in interpretation of ancient environments. Most of the sedimentary rocks, however, metamorphosed into biotite schist and biotite gneiss.

About 1,664 million years ago, a massive igneous intrusion occurred, today preserved as Boulder Creek Granodiorite and related pegmatites. The Boulder Creek batholith was the heat source for regional metamorphism. In a separate widespread intrusive episode, the granite of Hagues Peak (about 1,480 million years ago), mafic dikes (about 1,430 million years ago), and Silver Plume Granite and minor pegmatite (about 1,420 million years ago) were emplaced into the older biotite gneisses and schists throughout the Front Range. Deformation around these younger intrusions was localized but significant. For example, the near horizontal layering of banded schists and sheets of gray granite exposed in cirques east of the Continental Divide formed as Silver Plume Granite intruded into the older rocks and spread out laterally. Metamorphic effects related to the intrusions of Silver Plume Granite were relatively minor because the biotite gneisses and schists had already been recrystallized at high temperature and pressure.

Scientists do not know much about the Precambrian mountain ranges in which these rocks formed because they were worn away by erosion at the end of Precambrian time. The convoluted gneisses and schists, however, do tell us that Precambrian tectonic activity occurred repeatedly. Major faults produced during Precambrian events were later reactivated and play important roles in localizing mountain building in both Pennsylvanian and Laramide times.

Paleozoic and Mesozoic Eras

A long interval of erosion followed the metamorphic and igneous events of Precambrian time. Many thousands of feet of rock were removed, producing a major unconformity. Paleozoic seas crept across the area burying the ancient erosion surface with sediment. Little evidence remains in Rocky Mountain National Park of the more than 500 million years that comprise the Paleozoic and Mesozoic eras. Because of the lack of geologic clues within the park, geologists rely on upturned layers of sedimentary rock that lie outside the park's boundaries to learn what happened during this time.

Late Paleozoic mountain building (Pennsylvanian Period, about 300 million years ago) formed the Ancestral Rocky Mountains, which were elevated along some of the faults in the crystalline (Precambrian) basement. In general, the Paleozoic structures are not well preserved or are covered by later strata. Furthermore, in many areas where they are exposed, the possibility that later deformation reactivated and rotated these earlier structures cannot be completely ruled out (Kluth, 1997). Interpretation of the Ancestral Rocky

Mountains, therefore, is based on thickness, facies, and contact information within the sedimentary rocks deposited near the uplift during the orogeny (Kluth, 1997). The position of mountain uplift during Pennsylvanian time is coincident with the present-day Wet Mountains, Front Range, Medicine Bows, North Park Basin, Gore Range, and Park Range (Sonnenberg and Bolyard, 1997). As such, they extended from Boulder to Steamboat and were longer than the Front Range of today.

The area remained above sea level well into the Jurassic Period (about 150 million years ago). During this time, sediment deposition occurred in rivers, swamps, and dunes. These deposits are preserved outside of the park. By Cretaceous time, however, seas once again spread across the land. Evidence of the Cretaceous Interior Seaway is preserved in Rocky Mountain National Park in the form of Pierre Shale. The summits of Howard Mountain and Mount Cirrus in the Never Summer Mountains consist of this marine shale that was once mud at the bottom of the Late Cretaceous sea.

By the end of the Cretaceous Period and beginning of Tertiary Period (70 million years ago), the land was once again rising from the sea during a time of mountain building known as the Laramide orogeny. The events to follow consisted of a long series of repeated uplifts, periods of volcanism, and episodes of erosion (Richmond, 1974).

Cenozoic Era

The Laramide orogeny continued into the Cenozoic Era. The orogeny was a time of active tectonism and block-fault mountain building in Colorado (Sonnenberg and Bolyard, 1997). The deformation and uplift of the Laramide orogeny affected an area that had already been the site of large block uplift that formed the Ancestral Rocky Mountains (Kluth, 1997). Preexisting faults and shear zones largely controlled Laramide deformation (Sonnenberg and Bolyard, 1997). North-northwest-trending Precambrian faults control the north-northwest grain of the Front Range (Sonnenberg and Bolyard, 1997).

In addition to deformation expressed in the mountain uplifts, substantial Laramide deformation occurred in the bordering basins (Tweto, 1980a). These basins subsided concurrently with the uplift of the adjoining mountains. Each basin, e.g., the Denver, Raton, San Juan, Piceance, and Sand Wash, received Laramide orogenic sediments that constitute the principal record of events in the uplifts (Tweto, 1980b). Prior to uplift, thousands of feet of Paleozoic and Mesozoic sedimentary rocks overlay Precambrian crystalline rocks. Erosion, during and after the Laramide orogeny, removed the sedimentary rocks and some of the crystalline rocks from the range. The sedimentary rocks survive, however, in the flanking basins where they are commonly covered by Cenozoic rocks (Bradley, 1987).

Widespread volcanism affected most of the Southern Rocky Mountains in Oligocene time (Steven, 1975). The lava flows at Mount Richthofen mark an episode occurred 29.5 million years ago. Near Specimen Mountain, mudflows, lava flows, and obsidian are indicators of more recent activity (27.5 million years ago). In the Troublesome Formation (lower Miocene and upper Oligocene), lava flows in the lower units and ash beds in the upper units record volcanic activity 23 to 29 million years ago (Braddock and Cole, 1990). Volcanic ash is preserved as rhyolite welded tuff (late Oligocene) near Iceberg Lake along Trail Ridge Road. Volcanism was accompanied by igneous intrusion (Steven, 1975). The granite of Mount Cumulus stock (28.5 million years ago) is evidence of this.

A period of erosion continued after widespread Oligocene volcanism and eventually removed many of the volcanoes that formed in the Front Range area. Widespread fluvial deposition of volcanic and Precambrian clasts started in middle Miocene (14 to 11.5 million years ago); beds in the upper Troublesome Formation are evidence of this (Steven and others, 1997).

Broad uplift, block faulting, and erosion characterize Neogene (Miocene and Pliocene) time. Considerable scientific debate continues concerning the origin of the topographic difference between the mountains and flanking lowlands that formed during this time. Does the escarpment indicate Neogene faulting along the mountain front or is it caused by differential erosion of the rocks on opposite sides of the Laramide- age faults? Some evidence shows that nearly all of the modern relief along the eastern escarpment of the Front Range is due to differential erosion (Leonard and Langford, 1993). Other evidence, from the White River Plateau and Elkhead Mountains, suggests that there was nearly 2,000 feet (610 m) of offset during Neogene time (Tweto, 1980a). The debate continues, and new concepts and evidence are fueling the dialogue (e.g., Pederson and others, 2002).

The elevation of present- day mountains attests to Neogene events, as does a deposit in the park: a diamicton—unsorted, unstratified deposit—near Meeker Campground. This deposit is evidence of the Tertiary tectonic history in the area. The diamicton was deposited on a surface developed during Tertiary time that was later uplifted and deeply dissected (Wahlstrom, 1947; Madole, 1982).

The diamicton also played a role in interpreting the Quaternary glacial history of the area. The diamicton resembles till, but investigators have interpreted it as a fan deposit of Neogene or Quaternary age (Braddock and Cole, 1990), thereby having an alluvial origin, not a glacial one. This distinction is important because of the implications it has on Cenozoic climatic history. With respect to the location of this diamicton, if it were of glacial origin, early Pleistocene (i.e., pre- Bull Lake) glaciers must have been much larger than glaciers during later Bull Lake and Pinedale advances. A glacial interpretation of this diamicton goes against the overall pattern of glaciation documented thus far in the Front Range and neighboring ranges; that is, the extent of early and late Pleistocene glaciation was not notably different (Madole, 1976b).

The most recent regional tectonic event that influenced the Front Range was general uplift of the entire Southern Rocky Mountains, western Great Plains, and Colorado Plateau during the late Miocene and Pliocene, and possibly Quaternary time. Fault movement diminished after Pliocene time but continued on a minor scale through the Pleistocene and into the Holocene (Kirkham and Rodgers, 1981; Widmann and others, 1998). Uplift rejuvenated erosion and caused the long recognized "canyon cycle" (Lee, 1923) that cut deep canyons in the mountains. Canyon cutting probably continues today (Tweto, 1980a).

Uplift of nearly a mile (1.6 km) and worldwide cooling during the last few million years caused a profound transformation of climates. At times, winter snow at high elevations no longer completely melted during the summer but piled up in favorable locations, ultimately forming large valley glaciers. Although several glaciations occurred during Pleistocene time, geologists distinguish deposits of only three ages within or in close proximity to the boundaries of Rocky Mountain National Park. These glaciations are referred to as pre- Bull Lake, Bull Lake, and Pinedale. Investigators have identified deposits of Bull Lake and Pinedale glaciations in the park.

The glacial chronology of Rocky Mountain National Park is a work in progress. The beginning of the Bull Lake glaciation is based on correlations to marine isotope stage 6, which began about 180,000 years ago (Imbrie and others, 1984). Researchers estimated the timing using sea- surface temperature recorded in the oxygen- isotope compositions of the shells of foraminifera. Using oxygen isotopes, investigators date the end of the Bull Lake glaciation at 127,000 years ago (Bassinot and others, 1994). An interglacial (warm) period followed the Bull Lake glaciation, during which time Bull Lake glaciers completely melted away. Another glaciation followed for which there are good estimates of the timing of events. Using radiocarbon ages of organic-rich sediments at several high- elevation sites (Nelson and others, 1979; Madole, 1976b, 1980, 1986), investigators have estimated the timing of Pinedale glacial advances and retreats. Pinedale glaciation began about 30,000 years ago and was at its maximum between 23,500 and 21,000 years ago. Final deglaciation occurred between 15,000 and 12,000 years ago. Prior to 10,000 years ago, all Pinedale glaciers disappeared from the area. Pinedale glaciation was the last true valley glaciation to affect the Front Range.

Another glacial advance that occurred in late Pleistocene time is referred to as the Satanta Peak advance. This cirque- glacier advance was the most extensive to occur after the large valley glaciers disappeared. Researchers have documented this advance at Sky Pond in the park (Menounos and Reasoner, 1997). The Satanta Peak advance began prior to about 14,400 years ago and ended about 10,000 years ago (Rich Madole, written communication, 2003). The deposition of the Satanta Peak moraine in Loch Vale appears to be coeval with the European Younger Dryas event (Menounos and Reasoner, 1997).

Ice accumulation during Holocene time was not extensive enough to be considered an ice age. Some investigators have applied the term "Neoglaciation" to ice accumulation during the Holocene, but Neoglaciation may be a misnomer for the Front Range (Benedict, 1981). Post- Pleistocene ice accumulation is limited to within cirques. Investigators have identified many deposits in Rocky Mountain National Park, and deposits record four intervals of ice accumulation in the vicinity of the park. From oldest to youngest, they are referred to as Ptarmigan (7,250–6,380 BP), Triple Lakes (5,200–3,000 BP), Audubon (2,400–950 BP), and Arapaho Peak (350–100 BP) (Benedict, 1985). The Ptarmigan advance represents a brief reversal of the warming trend that had begun about 10,000 years ago (Benedict, 1985). The Triple Lakes accumulation was the most extensive. Arapaho Peak deposits are the Front Range equivalent of Little Ice Age moraines (Davis, 1988). Like modern glaciers, Audubon and Arapaho Peak glaciers depended on wind- drifted snow for their existence (Benedict, 1985).

Braddock and Cole (1990) identified 34 snow banks and ice masses in the vicinity of Rocky Mountain National Park. These include the snow and ice bodies shown on 1:24,000- scale topographic maps published between 1957 and 1962. Fourteen of the ice masses have been named: Rowe Glacier (between Rowe Peak and Hagues Peak), Sprague Glacier (at Irene Lake in Spruce Canyon), Tyndall Glacier (at the head of Tyndall Creek), Andrews Glacier (east of Andrews Pass), Taylor Glacier (at the head of Icy Brook), Chiefs Head Peak Glacier (above Frozen Lake), Mills Glacier (on the east side of Longs Peak), Moomaw Glacier (south of The Cleaver), and the six St. Vrain Glaciers (outside of the park at the head of Middle St. Vrain Creek).

All but one of these snow banks or ice masses are on the east side of the Continental Divide; the exception is the mass above Murphy Lake (near Snowdrift Peak). All but one occur at the heads of cirques: north- , northeast- , or east- facing; the exception is the large snowbank northeast of Rowe Mountain, which is in a northeast-facing gully. Some of the ice masses, such as Andrews Glacier, are actively moving and can be considered actual glaciers; others are stagnant. Winter winds—sometimes at velocities that exceed 200 miles (320 km) per hour—blow snow over the Continental Divide where it drifts into the Pleistocene- age cirques and nourishes some small glaciers. The process of snow deposition gives these "wind- drift glaciers" their name. It is not known whether, over a long period of time, these masses are growing or shrinking (Braddock and Cole, 1990).

The periglacial features that exist today are relicts of previous climatic conditions. Most of these features are not active today (Rich Madole, written communication, 2003). Features include patterned ground and other periglacial deposits on ridgetops and upland surfaces, tongue- shaped and lobate rock glaciers, and colluvium (e.g., talus and scree), alluvium (e.g., deposits at the margin of lateral moraines).

References Cited

Allen, T.J., 1936, Noteworthy geologic features in Rocky Mountain National Park, Colorado [unpublished memorandum to the Director (October 31, 1936), list of features, and appended bibliography]: U.S. Department of the Interior, National Park Service, 9 p.

Arps, L.W., and Kingery, E.E., assisted by Kingery, H.E., 1977, High country names—Rocky Mountain National Park and Indian Peaks: Boulder, Colorado, Johnson Books, published in cooperation with the Rocky Mountain Nature Association, 198 p. (Reprinted 1994.)

Bassinot, F.C., Labeyrie, L.D., Vincent, E., Quidelleur, X., and Shackleton, N.J., 1994, The astronomical theory of climate and the age of the Brunhes- Matuyama magnetic reversal: Earth and Planetary Science Letters, v. 126, p. 91–108.

Bates, R.L., and Jackson, J.A., eds., 1987, Glossary of geology (3rd ed.): Alexandria, Virginia, American Geological Institute, 788 p.

Benedict, J.B., 1970, Frost cracking in the Colorado Front Range: Geografiska Annaler, v. 52A, p. 87–93.

Benedict, J.B., 1981, The Fourth of July valley—glacial geology and archeology of the timberline ecotone: Ward, Colorado, Center for Mountain Archeology, Research Report No. 2, 139 p.

Benedict, J.B., 1985, Arapahoe Pass—glacial geology and archeology at the crest of the Colorado Front Range: Ward, Colorado, Center for Mountain Archeology, 197 p.

Berg, N.H., 1986, Blowing snow at a Colorado alpine site—measurement and implications: Arctic and Alpine Research, v. 18, p. 147–161.

Boos, C.M., and Boos, M.F., 1934, Granites of the Front Range—Longs Peak–St. Vrain batholith: Geological Society of America Bulletin, v. 45, p. 303–332.

Boos, M.F., and Boos, C.M., 1933, Iron Dike [abs.]: Geological Society of America Bulletin, v. 44, p. 73.

Braddock, W.A., and Cole, J.C., 1990, Geologic map of Rocky Mountain National Park and vicinity, Colorado: U.S. Geological Survey Map I- 1973, scale 1:50,000.

Braddock, W.A., and Peterman, Z.E, 1989, The age of the Iron Dike—a distinctive Middle Proterozoic intrusion in the northern Front Range of Colorado: The Mountain Geologist, v. 26, no. 4, p. 97–99.

Bradley, W.C., 1987, Erosion surfaces of the Colorado Front Range—a review, in Graf, W.L., ed., Geomorphic systems of North America: Boulder, Colorado, Geological Society of America, Centennial Special Volume 2, p. 215–220.

Caine, T.N., 1974, The geomorphic processes of the alpine environment, in Ives, J. D., and Barry, R.G., eds., Arctic and Alpine Environments: London, Methuen, p. 721–748.

Caine, T.N., 1986, Sediment and movement and storage on alpine slopes in the Colorado Rocky Mountains, in Abrahams, A.D., ed., Hillslope processes, The Binghamton Symposia in Geomorphology Series 16: Boston, Massachusetts, George Allen and Unwin, p. 115–137.

Chamberlain, R.T., 1919, The building of the Colorado Rockies: Journal of Geology, v. 27, p. 145–164, 225–251.

Cole, J.C., 1977, Geology of east- central Rocky Mountain National Park and vicinity, with emphasis on the emplacement of the Precambrian Silver Plume Granite in the Longs Peak–St. Vrain batholith [Ph.D. thesis]: Boulder, University of Colorado, 344 p.

Colorado Geological Survey, 1999, Where do diamonds come from?: RockTalk, v. 2, no. 3, p. 2–3.

Colton, R.B., Holligan, J.A., and Anderson, L.W., 1975, Preliminary map of landslide deposits, Greeley 1° X 2° quadrangle, Colorado: U.S. Geological Survey Miscellaneous Field Studies Map MF- 704, scale 1:250,000.

Cooper, D.J., Woods, S.W., Chimner, R.A., and MacDonald, L.H., 2000, Effects of the Grand Ditch on wetlands of the Kawuneeche Valley, Rocky Mountain National Park, Colorado: U.S. Department of the Interior, National Park Service, 373 p.

Davis, P.T., 1988, Holocene glacier fluctuations in the American Cordillera: Quaternary Science Reviews, v. 7, p. 21–38

Davis, W.M., 1911, The Colorado Front Range—as study in physiographic presentation: Association of American Geographers Annals, v. 11, p. 21–83.

Effinger, W.L., 1934, A report on the geology of Rocky Mountain National Park: Berkeley, California, Department of the Interior, National Park Service, Field Division of Education, 27 p.

Emerick, J.C., 1995, Rocky Mountain National Park natural history handbook: Niwot, Colorado, Roberts Rinehart Publishers, 158 p.

Epis, R.C., and Chapin, C.E., 1975, Geomorphic and tectonic implications of the post- Laramide, late Eocene erosion surface in the Southern Rocky Mountains, *in* Curtis, B.F., ed., Cenozoic history of the Southern Rocky Mountains: Geological Society of America Memoir 144, p. 45–74.

Fuller, M.B., 1924, General features of pre- Cambrian structure along the Big Thompson River in Colorado: The Journal of Geology, v. 32, no. 1, p. 49–63.

Fuller, M.B. 1926, Contact metamorphism in the Big Thompson schist in northcentral Colorado: American Journal of Science, v. 211, p. 194–200.

Gamble, B.M., 1979, Petrography and petrology of the Mount Cumulus Stock, Never Summer Mountains, Colorado [M.S. thesis]: Boulder, University of Colorado, 75 p.

Hopkins, R.L., and Hopkins, L.B., 2000, Hiking Colorado's geology: Seattle, The Mountaineers, 240 p.

Hoyt, W.H., 1987, A geologist's perspective of the 1982 Estes Park flood, *in* Gruntfest, E.C., ed., What we have learned since the Big Thompson Flood: Natural Hazards Research and Applications Information Center, Special Publication 16, p. 213–219.

Imbrie, J., Hays, J.D., Martinson, D.G., McIntyre, A., Mix, A.C., Morley, J.J., Pisias, N.G., Prell, W.L., and Shackleton, N.J., 1984, The orbital theory of Pleistocene climate—support from a revised chronology of the marine äi8O record, *in* Berger, A., Imbrie, J., Hayes, J., Kukla, G., and Saltzman, B., eds., Milankovitch and climate: Dordrecht, D. Reidel Publishing Co., pt. 1, p. 269–305.

International Conference of Building Officials, 1979, Uniform building codes (1979 edition).

Ives, J.D., and Fahey, B.D., 1971, Permafrost occurrence in the Front Range Colorado Rocky Mountains, U.S.A.: Journal of Glaciology, v. 10, p. 105–111.

Izett, G.A., 1974, Geologic map of the Trail Mountain quadrangle, Grand County, Colorado: U.S. Geological Survey Map GQ- 1156, scale 1:24,000.

Izett, G.A., 1975, Late Cenozoic sedimentation and deformation in northern Colorado and adjoining areas, *in* Curtis, B.F., ed., Cenozoic history of the Southern Rocky Mountains: Geological Society of America Memoir 144, p. 179–209.

Jarrett, R.D., 1987, Hydrologic research related to the 1976 Big Thompson River flood, Colorado, *in* Gruntfest, E.C., ed., What we have learned since the Big Thompson Flood: Natural Hazards Research and Applications Information Center, Special Publication 16, p. 203–212.

Jarrett, R.D., and Costa, J.E., 1986, Hydrology, geomorphology, and dam- break modeling of the July 15, 1982, Lawn Lake dam and Cascade Lake dam failures, Larimer County, Colorado: U.S. Geological Survey Professional Paper 1369, 78 p., 2 pls. in pocket.

Johnson, D., 1931, Planes and lateral corrosion: Science, v. 73, p. 174–177.

Johnson, D., 1932, Rock fans of arid regions: American Journal of Science, v. 23, p. 389–416.

Johnson, R.B., and Herzog, D.J., 1982, Summary of geologic factors that may influence the sensitivity of selected watersheds in Rocky Mountain National Park, Colorado, to atmospheric deposition: National Park Service, Water Resources Field Support Laboratory Report 82- 6, 23 p.

Kaye, G., 1983, Lulu City—Colorado River trail: Estes Park, Colorado, Rocky Mountain Nature Association, 14 p.

Kirkham, R.M., and Rogers, W.P., 1981, Earthquake potential in Colorado—a preliminary evaluation: Colorado Geological Survey Bulletin 43, 175 p.

Kiver, E.P., and Harris, D.V., 1999, Rocky Mountain National Park (Colorado), in Geology of U.S. Parklands (5th ed.): New York, John Wiley & Sons, chapt. 11, p. 630–644.

Kluth, C.F., 1997, Comparison of the location and structure of the Late Paleozoic and later Cretaceous–early Tertiary Front Range uplift, *in* Bolyard, D.W., and Sonnenberg, S.A., eds., Geologic history of the Colorado Front Range: Denver, Rocky Mountain Association of Geologists, p. 31–42.

Kron, D.G., 1988, Miocene mammals from the central Colorado Rocky Mountains [Ph.D. thesis]: Boulder, University of Colorado, 377 p.

Lee, W.T., 1923, Contributions to the geography of the United States, 1922—peneplains of the Front Range and Rocky Mountain National Park, Colorado: U.S. Geological Survey Bulletin 730, 17 p.

Leonard, E.M., and Langford, R.P., 1994, Post- Laramide deformation along the eastern margin of the Colorado Front Range—a case against significant faulting: The Mountain Geologist, v. 31, no. 2, p. 45–52.

Lewis, G.E., 1969, Larger fossil mammals and mylangaulid rodents from the Troublesome Formation (Miocene) of Colorado [Geological Survey Research 1969]: U.S. Geological Survey Professional Paper 650- B, p. B53–B56.

Lovering, T.S., 1930, The Granby anticline, Grand County, Colorado: U.S. Geological Survey Bulletin 822- B, p. 71–76.

Lovering, T.S., and Goddard, E.N., 1938, Mineralization and geology of proposed southern extension of Rocky Mountain National Park, Colorado [unpublished report]: U.S. Department of the Interior, National Park Service, 25 p.

Mackin, J.H., 1947, Altitude and local relief of the Bighorn area during the Cenozoic: Wyoming Geological Association, 2nd annual field conference, Guidebook, p. 103–120.

Madole, R.F., 1972, Neoglacial facies in the Colorado Front Range: Arctic and Alpine Research, v. 4, no. 2, p. 119–130.

Madole, R.F., 1976, Glacial geology of the Front Range, Colorado, in Mahaney, W.C., ed., Quaternary stratigraphy of North America: Stroudsburg, Pennsylvania, Dowden, Hutchinson, & Ross, Inc., p. 297–318.

Madole, R.F., 1980, Time of Pinedale deglaciation in north- central Colorado—further considerations: Geology, v. 8, p. 118–122.

Madole, R.F., 1982, Possible origins of till- like deposits near the summit of the Front Range in north- central Colorado: U.S. Geological Survey Professional Paper 1243, p. 1–31.

Madole, R.F., 1986, Lake Devlin and Pinedale glacial history, Front Range, Colorado: Quaternary Research, v. 25, p. 43–54.

Madole, R.F., VanSistine, D.P., and Michael, J.A., 1998, Pleistocene glaciation in the Upper Platte River drainage basin, Colorado: U.S. Geological Survey Geologic Investigations Series I- 2644, 1 pl.

Marvine, A.R., 1874, Report for the year 1873, in 7th annual report of the United States Geological and Geographical Survey of the Territories (Hayden's Survey): Washington, D.C., p. 83–192.

Matthews, V., KellerLynn, K., and Fox, B., 2003, Messages in stone—Colorado's colorful geology: Denver, Colorado Geological Survey, 157 p.

Meierding, T.C., and Birkeland, P.W., 1980, Quaternary glaciation of Colorado, in Kent, H.C. and Porter, K.W., eds., Colorado Geology: Denver, Rocky Mountain Association of Geologists, p. 165–173.

Menounos, B., and Reasoner, M.A., 1997, Evidence for cirque glaciation in the Colorado Front Range during Younger Dryas chronozone: Quaternary Research, v. 48, p. 38–47.

Merriman, M., 1960, Engineering geology—distribution system of the Colorado–Big Thompson Project, in Weimer, R.J., and Haun, J.D., eds., Guide to the geology of Colorado: Denver, Rocky Mountain Association of Geologists, p. 257–273.

Nelson, A.R., Millington, A.C., Andrews, J.T., and Nichols, H., 1979, Radiocarbon- dated upper Pleistocene glacial sequences, Fraser Valley, Colorado Front Range: Geology, v. 7, p. 410–414.

Outcalt, S.I., and Benedict, J.B., 1965, Photo- interpretation of two types of rock glacier in the Colorado Front Range, U.S.A.: Journal of Glaciology, v. 5, p. 849–856.

Pederson, J.L., Mackley, R.D., and Eddleman, J.L., 2002, Colorado Plateau uplift and erosion evaluated using GIS: GSA Today, v. 12, no. 8, p. 4–10.

Pearson, R.C., 1980, Mineral resources of the Indian Peaks study area, Boulder and Grand counties, Colorado: U.S. Geological Survey Bulletin 1463, 109 p.

Pitlick, J., 1993a, Geomorphic response of the Fall River, Rocky Mountain National Park, Colorado, in McCutchen, H.E., and Herrmann, R., eds., Ecological effects of the Lawn Lake flood of 1982, Rocky Mountain National Park, Scientific Monograph NPS/NRROMO/NRSM- 93/21: U.S. Department of the Interior, National Park Service, p. 18–32.

Pitlick, J., 1993b, Response and recovery of a subalpine stream following a catastrophic flood: Geological Society of America Bulletin, v. 105, p. 657–670.

Raup, O.B., 1996, Geology along Trail Ridge Road, Rocky Mountain National Park, Colorado: Helena and Billings, Montana, Falcon Press Publishing Company, 73 p.

Richmond, G.M., 1974, Raising the roof of the Rockies: Estes Park, Colorado, Rocky Mountain Nature Association, 81 p., 1 pl. in pocket.

Rocky Mountain National Park, Natural and cultural resources—environmental landscape, http://www.nps.gov/romo/resources/environment.html (accessed May 2004).

Seaman, D.M., 1934, Opal found at Specimen Mountain, Colorado: Portland, Oregon Mineralogist, v. 2, p. 12.

Shroba, R.R., Schmidt, P.W., Crosby, E.J., and Hansen, W.R., 1979, Geologic and geomorphic effects in the Big Thompson Canyon area, Larimer County, in Storm and flood of July 31–August 1, 1976, in the Big Thompson River and Cache La Poudre River basins, Larimer and Weld counties, Colorado: U.S. Geological Survey Professional Paper 1115, p. 87–148.

Sonnenberg, S.A., and Bolyard, D.W., 1997, Tectonic history of the Front Range of Colorado, in Bolyard, D.W., and Sonnenberg, S.A., eds., Geologic history of the Colorado Front Range: Denver, Rocky Mountain Association of Geologists, p. 1–7.

Steven, T.A., 1975, Middle Tertiary volcanic field in the Southern Rocky Mountains, *in* Curtis, B.F., ed., Cenozic history of the Southern Rocky Mountains: Geological Society of America Memoir 144, p. 75–94.

Steven, T.A., Evanoff, E., and Yuhas, R.H., 1997, Middle and late Cenozoic tectonic and geomorphic development of the Front Range of Colorado, *in* Bolyard, D.W., and Sonnenberg, S.A., eds., Geologic history of the Colorado Front Range: Denver, Rocky Mountain Association of Geologists, p. 115–124.

Street, F.A., 1973, A study of tors in the Front Range of the Rocky Mountains in Colorado, with special reference to their value as an indicator of non-glaciation [M.S. thesis]: Boulder, University of Colorado, 241 p.

Tweto, O., 1968, Geologic setting and interrelationships of mineral deposits in the mountain province of Colorado and south- central Wyoming, in Ore deposits of the United States, 1933–1967 (Graton Sales Volume): American Institute of Mining, Metallurgy, and Petroleum Engineers, no. 1, p. 551–588.

Tweto, O., 1980a, Tectonic history of Colorado, *in* Kent, H.C., and Porter, K.W., eds., Colorado Geology: Denver, Rocky Mountain Association of Geologists, p. 5–9.

Tweto, O., 1980b, Summary of Laramide orogeny in Colorado, *in* Kent, H.C., and Porter, K.W., eds., Colorado Geology: Denver, Rocky Mountain Association of Geologists, p. 129–134.

U.S. Department of the Interior, Bureau of Reclamation, Division of Dam and Structural Safety, 1982, SEED report on Bluebird dam, Pear dam, Sandbeach dam, Glacier No. 1 dam, Sprague Lake dam located within the boundary of Rocky Mountain National Park, Colorado: Denver, U.S. Department of the Interior, 103 p.

U.S. Department of the Interior, National Park Service, Division of Interpretive Planning, Harpers Ferry Center, 1985, Interpretive prospectus—Rocky Mountain National Park, Colorado: Rocky Mountain Regional Office, 67 p.

U.S. Department of the Interior, National Park Service, Land Resources Division, Mining and Minerals Branch, 1993, Lulu City area, Rocky Mountain National Park: [Lakewood, Colorado], Abandoned Mineral Lands Reclamation Program information sheet, 1 p.

Voynick, S.M., 1994, Colorado rockhounding—a guide to minerals, gemstones, and fossils: Missoula, Montana, Mountain Press Publishing Company, 372 p.

Wahlstrom, E.E., 1941, Hydrothermal deposits in the Specimen Mountain volcanics, Rocky Mountain National Park, Colorado: American Mineralogist, v. 26, p. 551–561.

Wahlstrom, E.E., 1947, Cenozoic physiographic history of the Front Range, Colorado: Geological Society of America Bulletin, v. 58, p. 551–572.

Wahlstrom, E.E., 1956, Petrology and weathering of the Iron Dike, Boulder and Larimer counties, Colorado: Geological Society of America Bulletin, v. 67, p. 147–163.

Wegemann, C.H., 1955, A guide to the geology of Rocky Mountain National Park [Colorado]: Washington, D.C, U.S. Department of the Interior, National Park Service, 32 p.

Widmann, B.L., Kirkham, R.M., and Rogers, W.P., 1998, Preliminary Quaternary fault and fold map and database of Colorado: Colorado Geological Survey Open File Report 98- 8, 331 p.

Appendix A: Geologic Map Graphic

This image provides a preview or "snapshot" of the digital geologic map for Rocky Mountain National Park which can be found on the included CD.

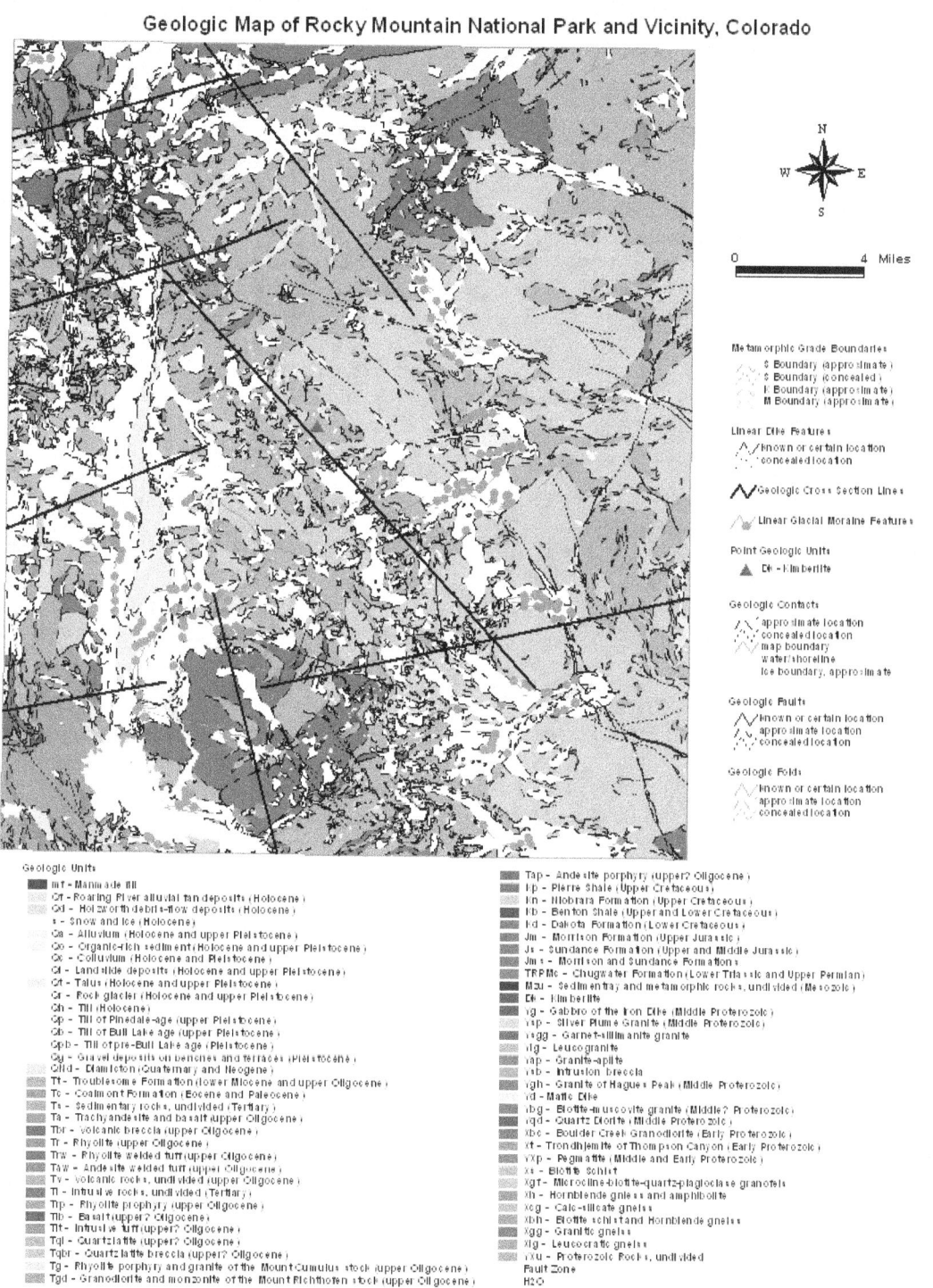

The original map digitized by NPS staff to create this product was: Braddock, W.A. and Cole, J.C., 1990, Geologic map of Rocky Mountain National Park and vicinity, Colorado, U.S. Geological Survey Miscellaneous Investigations Series Map I-1973, 1:50,000 scale. For a detailed digital geologic map and cross sections, see included CD.

Appendix B: Evaluation of Comprehensive Interpretive Plan (2001)

The geology of Rocky Mountain National Park is spectacular and readily accessible. "Geologic origins" and "glacial landscapes" have been repeatedly identified as important interpretive themes throughout the history of the park (e.g., Effinger, 1934; Allen, 1936; Wegemann, 1955; Interpretive prospectus [1985]).

General Comments

"Natural systems and processes" are mentioned in the Primary Interpretive Theme A of the draft of the comprehensive interpretive plan (CIP) for Rocky Mountain National Park (2001). It is assumed that this includes geology and geologic processes, but these important and primary themes have not received sufficient emphasis in this recent plan.

In addition, geology—the foundation for all other resources—is not directly identified in the section of the CIP listing resource- based issues that have been identified as important to interpret. Nitrate deposition is identified and is obviously geologically related with respect to wind- blown (aeolian) sediments. Water quality is also listed, and the interactions of both groundwater and surface water (i.e., rivers and streams, lakes and ponds, and wetlands) with soil and water- rock reactions (weathering) are well known. Nevertheless, these relationships may not be readily apparent to interpreters without a background in geology.

During a workshop that addressed the CIP, stakeholders identified "the Woman's ROMO" as an important topic to interpret. With respect to geology, a woman was the first person to conduct a systematic study of the area's structure and metamorphism. Margaret Bradley Fuller, who later changed her name to Boos after marriage, studied the metasedimentary rocks east of Estes Park in the Big Thompson Canyon (1924, 1926). She also did work on the Iron Dike (1933), after which she and her husband published the results of a reconnaissance on the granites of the Front Range (Boos and Boos, 1934).

Interpreting geology is challenging, particularly for those interpreters who have not been trained in the subject. It takes an awareness of the importance of geology to the park setting, human history, present landscape, and present species to insist on doing it, but it can be done. Publications, the park's Web site, interpretive facilities, and interdivisional communication are areas that could benefit from the inclusion of geology.

Publications

Use portions of this report for interpretive materials

The CIP for Rocky Mountain National Park identified the need to update interpretive publications, specifically on geology (p. 10). The Geologic Features and Processes section of this report could be adapted for a site bulletin. This report (or portions of it) could be reformatted for general audience and published through the Rocky Mountain Nature Association.

Insure the availability of geologic publications in cooperating association bookstores

Many national parks have publications available for visitors on their park's geology. On October 16, 2002, this was not the case for Beaver Meadows Visitor Center in Rocky Mountain National Park. Some suggested publications for distribution to the general public are:

Braddock, W.A., and Cole, J.C., 1990, Geologic map of Rocky Mountain National Park and vicinity, Colorado: U.S. Geological Survey Map I- 1973, scale 1:50,000.

Hopkins, R.L. and Hopkins, L.B., 2000, Hiking Colorado's geology: Seattle, The Mountaineers, 240 p.

Matthews, V., KellerLynn, K., and Fox, B. 2003. Messages in stone—Colorado's colorful geology: Denver, Colorado Geological Survey, 157 p.

Consider reprinting certain geologic publications

Other good publications on the geology of the park have gone out of print. Two books in particular are worth consideration for reprinting:

Raup, O.B., 1996, Geology along Trail Ridge Road, Rocky Mountain National Park, Colorado: Helena and Billings, Montana, Falcon Press Publishing Company, 73 p., 1 pl.

Richmond, G.M., 1974, Raising the roof of the Rockies: Estes Park, Colorado, Rocky Mountain Nature Association, 81 p., 1 pl. in pocket.

Web site

Use NPS "Views" as a model for park's Web site

The CIP identified a needed upgrade of the park's Web site (p. 17). The Internet is a wonderful place to post information about the park's natural resources, including geologic resources. "Views of the National Park Service, Virtual Experiences, and Knowledge Centers" could serve as a model for Rocky Mountain National Park.

Interpretive Facilities

Incorporate geology into Alpine Visitor Center exhibit

The exhibit at the Alpine Visitor Center that needs to be renovated could include a geology theme. The geomorphic processes and geologic features that occur at high elevations in the park are readily visible and easily interpreted. They are distinctive and visited by millions of people each year. They include: potential hazards such as solifluction and frost cracking, solifluction terraces, patterned ground (e.g., rock polygons, rock stripes, rock circles, felsenmeer), uplifted erosion surfaces (an interesting and yet not fully explained geologic story), tors, and sackung features. (Please refer to the Geologic Features and Processes section and Geologic Issues section of this report for explanations.)

Incorporate geology into Hidden Valley nature trail

As the Hidden Valley area is redeveloped, a nature trail should to be planned. An interesting story links human influences and geologic processes. Workers buried the stream channel in Hidden Valley and placed culverts during construction of the lodge at the ski area. Diversion of streamflow for winter recreation also impacted this small watershed. For several decades, streamflow was diverted for making artificial snow at the ski resort. Human alteration of streamflow in this watershed may have caused significant impacts to the aquatic habitat, including the stream channel and wetlands, and may have affected many lifecycles, including that of the threatened greenback cutthroat trout *(Oncorhynchus clarki stomias)*. Evaluation and documentation of human alteration and its effects could be developed into an interpretive message. The story to be told is that of impact and restoration of the natural (geologic) system.

Hidden Valley is also a site where the Iron Dike outcrops. The accessibility of the Iron Dike provides the opportunity to tell an ancient story about the Precambrian history of the park. It also provides an opportunity to educate visitors about the role of bedrock composition on soil chemistry and its influence on vegetation and animal species.

Interdivisional Communication

Insist on peer review of scientific information prior to dissemination

"Given the new emphasis on research in Rocky Mountain National Park, it is critical that the interpretive program be infused with the latest information on current issues and research" (CIP, p. 19). Also critical is that park staff develops a process that insures that the information gained from scientific research is "good science." The process should include peer review by appropriate scientists to verify the accuracy of the information before being released to the public (or media) in either oral or written form. The NPS Geologic Resources Division could facilitate outside reviews by appropriate organizations and individuals.

Get needed geologic expertise

The transfer of information from researchers to park staff and the public is necessary for making sound decisions and to enhance the understanding (and enjoyment) of park resources. The CIP identified "geologic topics" as research needs for the park (p. 15), specifically the need for high- quality research on the formation of the Rockies.

Because the park does not have a geologist on staff, the Interpretation Division is encouraged to submit a proposal for the Geoscientists- in- the- Parks (GIP) program. Geoscientists at all points in their careers participate in this program, and all levels of expertise may be requested. Rocky Mountain National Park received funding for a GIP in 2001. This project and the media attention that it received increased interest of the geoscience community to conduct research in the park (Terry Terrell, oral communication, 2002). A lesson learned from this is that interesting geologic research is waiting to be conducted in Rocky Mountain National Park; park managers simply need assistance in identifying projects. The GIP program manager can assist in drafting the short proposal. The potential project to be completed may simply be to identify needed geologic research for making management decisions or a review of current interpretive materials on the park's geology.

Rocky Mountain National Park
Geologic Resource Evaluation Report

Natural Resource Report NPS/NRPC/GRD/NRR—2004/004
NPS D-307, September 2004

National Park Service
Director • Fran P. Mainella

Natural Resource Stewardship and Science
Associate Director • Michael A. Soukup

Natural Resource Program Center
The Natural Resource Program Center (NRPC) is the core of the NPS Natural Resource Stewardship and Science Directorate. The Center Director is located in Fort Collins, with staff located principally in Lakewood and Fort Collins, Colorado and in Washington, D.C. The NRPC has five divisions: Air Resources Division, Biological Resource Management Division, Environmental Quality Division, Geologic Resources Division, and Water Resources Division. NRPC also includes three offices: The Office of Education and Outreach, the Office of Inventory, Monitoring and Evaluation, and the Office of Natural Resource Information Systems. In addition, Natural Resource Web Management and Partnership Coordination are cross-cutting disciplines under the Center Director. The multidisciplinary staff of NRPC is dedicated to resolving park resource management challenges originating in and outside units of the national park system.

Geologic Resources Division
Chief • David B. Shaver
Planning Evaluation and Permits Branch Chief • Carol McCoy

Credits
Author • Katie KellerLynn
Editing • Sid Covington
Digital Map Production • Stephanie O'Meara and Jenny Adams
Map Layout Design • Melanie Ransmeier

www.ingramcontent.com/pod-product-compliance
Lightning Source LLC
Chambersburg PA
CBHW080350290526
45791CB00009BA/2818